PASSPORT

Mexican Caribbean

PHOTO O F NEW CITIZEN
OF THE MEXICAN
CARIBBEAN

DATE OF VISIT TO THE
MEXICAN CARIBBEAN:

Passport Number:

HOLDER'S SIGNATURE

NAMES

SURNAME

NATIONALITY

—CITIZEN OF THE MEXICAN CARIBBEAN—

DATE OF BIRTH

SEX _____

The bearer hereby declares him/herself to be a citizen of the Mexican
Caribbean, a connoisseur of its turquoise sea, its mysterious cenotes
and its seven-hued lagoons. He/she proclaims him/herself to be
a defender of its exotic nature, its sea turtles and its legendary
manatees, and he/she confesses an enduring admiration for the
enigmatic cities of the Ancient Maya, legacy of a culture that still
lives in this wonderful corner of the planet.

PASSPORT

Mexican Caribbean

Contents

"Where are we?"
"Under Mexican skies, in front of the Caribbean Sea, in the beautiful state of Quintana Roo."
"Just give me the geography."
"Write this down: we're between latitude 21° 35' to the north and 17° 49' to the south; and longitude 86° 42' to the east and 89° 25' to the west.
"OK. Now I won't get lost."

"You can't get lost. To the north, we have the state of Yucatan and the Gulf of Mexico; to the east is the Caribbean Sea, to the south is the Bay of Chetumal, Belize and Guatemala; and to the west are the states of Campeche and Yucatan. The capital is the beautiful city of Chetumal." "So how big is the State?"

"Quintana Roo is 19,492 square miles. Almost all of it is untouched nature."

"Really?"

"And I'll tell you something else! There are 373 miles of sunsets!"

"Sunsets?"

"Coastline, where you get the most beautiful sunsets in the world!"

YUCA

XLAPAK

GULF OF
MEXICO

CAMPECHE

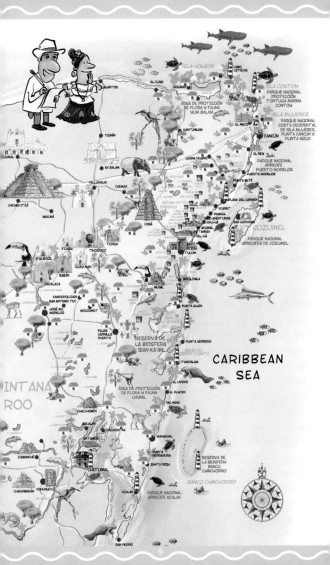

A sun on the coat of arms

"Did you see the sun? It's the first thing you notice on the coat of arms."

"You have to have the rising sun, with its ten golden rays for the ten municipalities in the State!"

"And underneath the sun?"

"A shell and a five-point star."

"And below them?"

"Three triangles above the Mayan glyph for wind, in emerald green. All the coat of arms represents Quintana Roo."

"It looks even prettier now that I understand it."

Anthem of Quintana Roo

"Listen to the anthem. The words were written by Ramón Iván Suárez Caamal, with music by Marco A. Ramírez Canul in 1985. In the five verses and the chorus you can hear the origin of our people, the struggles for land and the birth of the State, which is the youngest in Mexico."

"I'm all ears."

I

Chorus
Forest, sea, history and youth,
A free and just people under the sun,
Tenacity their virtue:
That is Quintana Roo!

From the deep roots of the Maya
To the resolve that builds the present,
With head held high we sing,
In anthem, fraternal loyalty.

Its notes ring in harmony
And the voice of your people enfolds you,
The clamor of the jungle repeats it
And the turmoil of the sea sings it.

Forest, sea, history and youth,
A free and just people under the sun,
Tenacity their virtue:
That is Quintana Roo!

II

On your arms the dawn salutes
As it rises from the tempestuous Caribbean
For on your soil the Motherland receives
The first caress of the sun.

Ten rays are your municipalities,
Ten rays of light ascending,
The past becomes present
In the glyph of your shell.

Forest, sea, history and youth,
A free and just people under the sun,
Tenacity their virtue:
That is Quintana Roo!

III

This land that faces east
Was cradle of the mestizos
Born of the honorable love
Between Gonzalo Guerrero and *Za'asil.*

The force of the wind does not bow you,
Nor does brute ambition divide you
Your giant stature is measured
In the pact of federal union.

Forest, sea, history and youth,
A free and just people under the sun,
Tenacity their virtue:
That is Quintana Roo!

IV

In Tepich the courage of the Maya
Turned oppression into victory,
The machete wrote in our history:
Liberty! Liberty! Liberty!

Santa Cruz was sanctuary to the free,
His refuge: the jungle and the swamp
For the Indian arose against the tyrant,
A hounded boar, a jaguar.

Forest, sea, history and youth,
A free and just people under the sun,
Tenacity their virtue:
That is Quintana Roo!

V

Manna is the latex from the
wounded wood,
The sea gives up its treasures to the net,
The beehive its tears of gold
And the land its fruits in season.

Work is the strength of a people
For it makes life more worthy,
To build is the noble watchword
And to be free the eternal choice.

Forest, sea, history and youth,
A free and just people under the sun,
Tenacity their virtue:
That is Quintana Roo!

A young State

"So how long has Quintana Roo been a State of Mexico?"

"Since 1974, when it stopped being a Federal Territory. At that time seven of its ten municipalities were created."

"And the other three?"

"The eighth was Solidaridad, created in 1993. Then *Tulum*, in 2008, and finally Bacalar in 2011."

YUCATÁN

GULF OF
MEXICO

JOSÉ
MARÍA
MORELOS

OTHÓN P
BLANCO

ISLA
MUJERES

LÁZARO
CÁRDENAS

BENITO
JUÁREZ

SOLIDARIDAD

TULUM

COZUMEL

XelHa

CARIBBEAN
SEA

FELIPE CARRILLO
PUERTO

BACALAR

Tropical heat

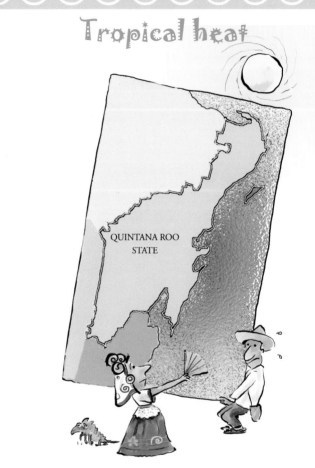

QUINTANA ROO
STATE

"It's hot here!"
"What did you expect? We're in the tropics! The average maximum temperature is 91° F, between March and October."

"All I know is that in May and June the only thing you want is to spend all day in the sea."

"The climate in Quintana Roo is warm sub-humid, with an average temperature of 79° F. But don't complain – it's a great climate for sugarcane, habanero chilis, and fruit like sapodilla, orange, lime, mango and pineapple."

"Does it rain?"

"Almost all year. Enough to keep our vegetation green all the time."

A limestone plain

"Quintana Roo is a plain, in the Yucatan peninsula."

"Everyone knows that."

"What you didn't know is that this peninsula rose out of the sea millions of years ago. That's why it's full of fossil shells and underground rivers."

"What an exotic State!"

"It's a jungle, with flat plain in the north and east, and some hills to the west, formed of sedimentary rocks. There we have the highest point: the Cerro de Chinos is 1,214 feet above sea level. The ground is so calcareous that the Ancient Maya used to build their monuments with a material called *sascab*, leaving kind of cavern-quarries called *sascaberas*."

"Is that why the rain water filters through?"

"Yes. It forms rivers and deposits of underground

water, like cenotes (sink holes)."
"Cenotes?"
"I'll tell you about Quintana Roo's natural
beauties later."

Liquid treasures
Underground rivers and lagoons

"Quintana Roo has the largest network of underground rivers in the world, and one of the most important reserves of fresh water in Mexico. The main mouth of these rivers is at **Xel-Há**. There are also lagoons like the ones at Bacalar, San Felipe, *Kaná y Nichupté*."

"Do all the rivers go underground?"

"Not all of them: the Río Hondo is a natural border with Belize, and its tributary, the Río Azul, is also a border with Guatemala."

"And there's me thinking there's no water here."

"There's plenty of water. The inlet at **Xcaret**, the old port of *Polé*, also receives fresh water from several underground rivers."

GULF OF
MEXICO

TÁN

ISLA HOLBOX

YALAHAU

ISLA
CONTOY

EL MECO
LAGUNA
NICHUPTÉ

ISLA
MUJERES

EL REY

L. YODZONOT

L. PUNTA
LAGUNA

XCARET
PAAMUL
XPU-HÁ
AKUMAL

SAN GERVASIO

COZUMEL

COBÁ

XEL-HÁ
TANKAH
TULUM

MUYIL
CATOCHE

LAGUNA
KANTEMÓ

BAHÍA DE
LA ASCENSIÓN

L. DZINZANTÚN

L. OCOM

L. KANÁ

BAHÍA DEL
ESPÍRITU SANTO

L. PAYTORO

L. SAC AYÍN

L. NOHBEC

QUINTANA
ROO

DOS OROS

CARIBBEAN
SEA

CHACCHOBÉN

L. LAGARTO

LAGUNA
BACALAR

OXTANKAH

LAGUNA
CHAKANBAKÁN

DZIBANCHÉ   RÍO UCUM

L. SAN JOSÉ
AGUILAR

KOHUNLICH

CHAKANBAKÁN

BAHÍA DE
CHETUMAL

RÍO HONDO

BANCO CHINCHORRO

RÍO AZUL

BELICE

21

Bacalar Lagoon

"Hold on to the boat!"

"Bacalar... Where does such a pretty name come from?"

"From the Mayan words *Bak Halal*, which means "place surrounded by reeds"."

"The last thing I care about is reeds. Do you see how beautiful the lagoon is?"

"It's not called "Seven-Colored Lagoon" for nothing".

"It has got seven colors. Can you see them?"

"Of course I can! There are seven different shades of blue!"

"A real natural spectacle!"

Río Hondo

"How deep is this river?"
"84 of its 96 miles are navigable, and there are stretches where it's extremely deep. It starts in Guatemala, where it's called Río La Palma, it forms the frontier between Mexico and Belize, and then flows into Chetumal Bay."
"It looks very wide here in Quintana Roo."
"It forms a lot of lagoons in all the shades of blue you can imagine."
"Ah! So that's why in some stretches it's called the Blue River."
"On the way to Chetumal it sometimes flows underground and makes cenotes, like the Cenote Azul."
"How much history the Río Hondo must have seen!"
"It's seen the Maya, the Mestizos, and even the Mennonites, not to mention pirates like Wallace the Scot, who smuggled logwood."
"Look! There are iguanas, snakes and alligators."
"And deer, pheasants, quetzals and toucans."
"The Rio Hondo is certainly worth getting to know!"

Land of Cenotes
Wonders of Quintana Roo

"The word "cenote" comes from the Maya *dzonot*, which means a cavern with water."

"And are they all like that, caves?"

"There are open ones, semi-open and cave or closed ones."

"How are they formed?"

"They start as underground chambers that appear when the limestone rock is dissolved by rainwater and underground rivers. Little by little, the cavity gets bigger, until it gets exposed to the surface when the roof collapses."

"Do they take a long time to form?"

"They were formed during the Pleistocene, and they're typical of the Yucatan peninsula. There are similar cenotes on the Nullarbor Plain, and there are the famous "Blue Holes" in the Bahamas."

"But the ones here are the most beautiful!"

"There are cenotes like Sac Actún (the Gran Cenote), which has been declared "the longest sub aquatic cave in the world", where they've found remains of primitive man and prehistoric animal skeletons."

"Who would have thought it?"

"There are other incredibly beautiful ones, like the Cenote Azul, the Cenote Dos Ojos, the Ponderosa and all the ones along the "Cenote Route.""

"There's a Cenote Route?"

"Here they are Nature's gift."

Prehispanic Cenotes

"For the Maya, the cenotes were a source of life, ritual places. They were part of the Underworld or *Xibalbá*, so they used them as natural funeral chambers."

"How do we know they were tombs, and not prehistoric fossils?"

"Because of the funeral treatment accompanying the skeletons: they were surrounded by vases and sacrificed animals. They've found these remains in two cenotes."

"Which ones?"

"In the Sacred Cenote at *Chichén Itzá* and in Las Calaveras Cenote, where they found remains in 2007."

TYPES OF CENOTES

"Where is Las Calaveras?"
"Here at *Tulum*, Quintana Roo. It might be the best-preserved Ancient Maya burial site. It has a lot of human skeletons in very good condition, together with the offerings that they were buried with."
"I hadn't heard of that discovery!"
"It's very important. It'll allow genetic and anthropological studies that will tell us more about the Ancient Maya who lived here."
"What time are they from?"
"They think from between 125 and 236 AD."
"Our ancestors are still full of surprises!"

Prehistoric Cenotes

"Prehistoric Cenotes?"

"Believe it or not, they've explored nine underwater cave systems, two in Yucatan and seven in Quintana Roo. They've found skeletons there from the end of the Ice Age, at least 10,000 years ago."

"That's around the Pleistocene!"

"It's the end of the Pleistocene and the beginning of our era, called the Holocene."

"Are they really that old?"

"They're so old that people are rethinking the theories about the arrival of the first humans in the Yucatan peninsula. Fortunately, caves are ideal for preserving organic remains, otherwise there wouldn't even be bones."

"And what caves did they turn up in?"

"At the bottoms of the caverns called Naharon, Las Palmas, El Templo and Chan-Hol, they found four nearly complete human skeletons: two women, one man, and one that hasn't been identified yet."

The group is known as the "Naharon Woman's Gang". The name comes from the cave where they found the first skeleton, a woman about 20 years old."

"Didn't they find any animals?"

"There were remains of extinct mammals of the Pleistocene, like horses (*Equus conversidens*), camels (*Hemiauchenia macrocefala*), elephants (*Gonphoterium sp*) and giant armadillos (*Glypotherium cf. G floridanum*)."

"How did they get there?"

"These caves were flooded at the end of the Ice Age, when enormous ice sheets melted, raising the sea level. Humans, animals and plants remained trapped until now."

"Those explorations are going to bring interesting news. As for me, I prefer to dive in the shallows. I don't want to end up a research specimen in the future."

The Cenotes Route

"Where are we?"

"In Leona Vicario, where the Santa Maria Hacienda used to be, in the golden age of gum."

"What does that have to do with cenotes?"

"To get the gum out and ship it for export, they built a rail track from the hacienda to Punta Corcho, today Puerto Morelos."

"You still haven't told me what that has to do with cenotes."

"Today, the Leona Vicario–Central Vallarta–Puerto Morelos route goes past several cenotes, so it's called the "Cenote Route"."

"And what's special about it?"

"We can see one by one the cenotes that form part of the most important underground river system in the world. The ecological diversity of this region is based on this hidden reserve of water."

"Can you swim in them?"

"Not only swim. You can visit and enjoy the exuberant jungle around them."

"Do they have names?"

"The ones you can visit are Las Mojarras, Verde Lucero, Boca del Puma, Siete Bocas, Tres Bocas, *Kin Há*, La Noria, La Orquídea, Salsipuedes, Paraíso, Agua Azul and San Martiniano."

ISLA HOLBOX

CABO CATOCHE

EL CUYO   HOLBOX

KANTUNILKIN

EL MECO

LEONA VICARIO

CANCÚN

MÍN

EL REY

VICENTE GUERRERO

LA ORQUÍDEA

SAN LORENZO

TRES BOCAS

BALAM

AGUA AZUL

DELRÍOS   EL PARAÍSO

CENTRAL VALLARTA

PUERTO MORELOS

SAN MARTINIANO

PUNTA BETÉ

GUADALUPE VICTORIA

CHEMAX

PLAYA DEL CARMEN

XCARET

COBÁ

PAAMUL

RÍO AVENTURAS

XPU-HÁ

SAN GERVASIO

AKUMAL

XEL-HÁ

EPICH

TANKAH

TULUM

COZUMEL

BOCA PAILA

MUYIL

PUNTA ALLEN

BAHÍA DE LA ASCENSIÓN

Cenotes on The Mayan Riviera

"The Mayan Riviera is full of cenotes!"

"All together?"

"They're almost all open-type, and they're grouped alongside the Cancun-*Tulum* highway."

"Can you dive in them?"

"For real scuba-diving you have to go with an expert guide, and only in some cenotes, like Chikin Ha, Dos Ojos and Gran Cenote. But what you can do is dive with a snorkel and visor."

"Let's go then!"

"In the cenotes you can see fish like catfish, bream, blind fish (*Ogilbia pearsei* and *Ophisternon infernale*) and several species of crustacean."

"And how many cenotes are there?"

"Loads, but a lot of them are in the middle of the jungle, and it's almost impossible to get to them. There are supposed to be over 15,000 cenotes in the Yucatan peninsula, counting open and closed ones."

"Let's go see them."

"You won't regret it."

JOSÉ MA. MORELOS

CABO
CATOCHE

ISLA
CONTOY

EL MECO

ISLA
MUJERES

CANCÚN

EL REY

PUERTO
MORELOS

PUNTA
BETÉ

CENOTE
AZUL

KUKULCÁN
CHAC MOOL

PLAYA
DEL CARMEN

XCARET

CRISTALINO

CHI KIN HÁ

PAAMUL

PTO AVENTURAS

XPU-HÁ

SAN GERVASIO

COZUMEL

COBÁ

TAJ MAHA
DOS OJOS
GRAN CENOTE
IAKTUN HÁ
GALAVERA

AKUMAL

XEL-HÁ

TANKAH

CRISTAL
ESCONDIDO
ANGELITA

TULUM

MUYIL

CENOTE
AZUL

PUNTA ALLEN

CENOTE
CHAN DZONOT

BAHÍA DE
LA ASCENCIÓN

CARIBBEAN
SEA

FORMATION OF A CENOTE

VAULTED CAVERN WHOSE
ROOF HAS NOT FALLEN.

SEMI-COLLAPSED
VAULT.

ROOF ALMOST COMPLETELY
COLLAPSED.

TYPICAL VERTICAL-SIDED
CENOTE.

ERODED WALLS.

CENOTE OR "WATER-HOLE" WITH
A SPRING AT THE BOTTOM.

Cenotes in the Southern Region
Cenote Azul

"This is one cenote you'll never forget."

"But this is a lagoon!"

"It's the Bacalar Lagoon. Over there, just 100 yards from the coast, is the Cenote Azul. This cenote is a must-see for the divers who visit Quintana Roo."

"The vegetation around it is wonderful just by itself."

"You can't imagine the experience when you dive in it. There are mazes of roots and tree trunks, incredible caves and almost vertical rock formations."

"Let's go in!"

"We'll go with an expert guide. This cenote is 300 feet deep."

"Gulp! Don't let go of me!"

"That's what I told the guide."

A forest state
Jungle and coast in Quintana Roo

"Do you know all the trees that grow here?"
"Do I know them? Two-thirds of the trees in the State produce fine woods."
"Really?"
"The jungle is full of red cedar, mahogany, *ceiba*, rosewood, *tzalán* (wild tamarind), *jabín* (Jamaican dogwood), *chobenché* (broomstick), *pucté* (black olive), granadillo, guayacán and oak; there's also ebony, *huizache* (needle bush) and *huanacaxtle* (elephant ear tree).
"And the sapodilla (*Manilkara zapota*)?"
"It provides wood, and it's one of the most important trees because that's where they get the

CHIIT

RAMÓN

CHACÁH

resin that makes chewing gum. It's all exported."

"Wow!"

"There are fruit trees like the caimito (*Chrysophyllum mexicanum*) and the guaya (*Talisia olivaeformis*)."

"And what trees are there on the coast?"

"The Sea Grape (*Coccoloba uvifera*), siricote (Geiger Tree) (*Cordia sebestena*) and of course the red mangrove (*Rhyzophora mangle*)."

Dr. Alfredo Barrera Marín Botanical garden

"It's in the north of the State, the municipality of Benito Juárez, on the Puerto Morelos-Playa del Carmen highway. There are 160.62 acres of vegetation, which makes it one of the largest in the country."

"It's so quiet and peaceful!"

"You can see two types of natural vegetation here: the evergreen seasonal forest, the trees that lose their leaves during the dry season, and the red mangrove (*Rizophora mangle*)."

"I can also see trees that are typical of Quintana Roo's flora: the sapodilla (*Manilkara zapota*), the breadnut (*Brosimum alicastrum*), the guaya (*Talisia olivaeiformis*), chiit (thatch palm) (*Thrinax radiata*) and nacax (silver palm) (*Cocothrinax readii*).

"You can find iguanas here, birds of all colors, and spider monkeys."

Traditional medicine

"In Quintana Roo the traditions of the Mayan world are still alive. Mother earth provides what you need to live, and even to heal you."

"What is traditional medicine like?"

"It's made up of lots of healing techniques, with rituals and of course it uses traditional herbal remedies."

"Do people still get treated that way?"

"Yes. Many Mayan communities practice it."

"Do you know the properties of plants?"

"Some of them. This one is called *Kanan* (Firebush) (*Amelia patens*) in Maya."

"And this one?"

"That's guarumbo (*Cecropia obtucifolia*). It's good for fighting diabetes. But it's better if I give you a list of the most commonly used medicinal plants."

"If you have one for lovesickness, let me know."

Wetlands

"What are wetlands?"

"They're areas of flooded land which are almost always in between the sea and the jungle. They might be savanna, petenes, tacistales (two kinds of tree-islands) or the best-known are the mangrove swamps. All wetlands can be fresh water, salt water, or a mixture."

"Are there a lot of them?"

"One of the most important wetlands is here in Quintana Roo: the *Sian Ka'an* Reserve. The water in this wetland comes from rain, from the cenotes and underground rivers that connect with the surface via springs."

"Why are they important?"
"That's a silly question! The wetlands are natural water filters. They're a habitat for many species of fish, and they keep our famous coral reef fed with nutrients."
"Why are the mangrove swamps better-known?"
"Because they're a source of all sorts of life. Although people associate them with bad smells, mosquitoes and dangerous animals like crocodiles and snakes; there are actually a lot of permanent and migratory species that live there. They are breeding grounds, a guarantee for wildlife."
"All that? I'll look at wetlands in a different light from now on."

Wildlife
Wealth of land and sea

FOUREYE BUTTERFLYFISH

RAINBOW PARROTFISH

LOOKDOWN

SERGEANT MAJOR

"Wildlife is abundant here, you know."

"I've seen mammals like howler monkeys, armadillos, white-tailed deer and raccoons."

"There are also tapirs, skunks, wild boar, pacas, chipmunks, bats and even the famous manatees, which are in danger of extinction."

"And birds of all colors."

"Toucans, cardinals, pheasants, chachalacas and parrots. There were also macaws in the southwest of the State."

BLUE TANG
SURGEONFISH

"And snakes like the rattlesnake, the boa and the coral snake."
"And there are crocodiles in the mangrove swamps!"
"And herons and turtles."
"On the coast and out to sea there are sharks, grouper, tarpon, red snapper, dogfish, conch and black coral."
"You're right, there's wildlife everywhere."
"It's the wildlife suited to this climate and this kind of vegetation."

FAIRY BASSLET

BLUESTRIPED GRUNT

BLUE ANGELFISH

The Great Mesoamerican Reef System

"Whaaat system?"

"The Great Mesoamerican Reef System, or the Great Mayan Reef. It's an ecosystem unique in the western hemisphere, over a six hundred miles long! It's the second largest in the world, after the Great Barrier Reef in Australia."

"A Mexican system!"

"It starts in Mexico, at Cabo Catoche in the north of Quintana Roo, then it goes past Belize and Guatemala and ends in Honduras."

"And what's in this reef system?"

"Everything: fringing reefs, barrier reefs and atolls, keys, islands, coastal wetlands, reef lagoons and coastal lagoons, prairies of seaweed, even mangrove forests! They are the Earth's lungs, producing great quantities of oxygen and food for turtles, manatees, sea urchins, surgeon fish and parrot fish, among others."

"I know the Coral Reef Aquarium at **Xcaret**."

"It's an extraordinary educational project at **Xcaret** Park, where you can see reefs just as they are at sea, to raise awareness in the younger generations about the preservation of life in the coral reef."

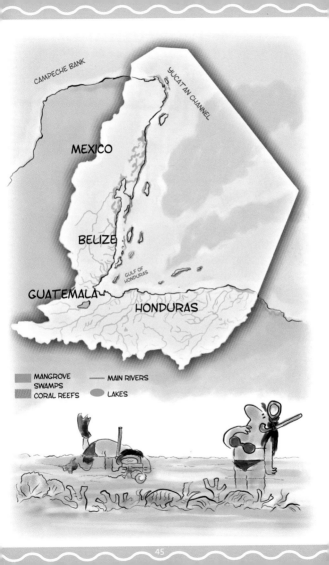

CAMPECHE BANK

YUCATAN CHANNEL

MEXICO

BELIZE

GULF OF HONDURAS

GUATEMALA

HONDURAS

MANGROVE SWAMPS

CORAL REEFS

MAIN RIVERS

LAKES

Marine turtles

"What are you doing?"

"Shh! I'm waiting for the marine turtles."

"On land? But they're sea animals!"

"Yes, but the adult female comes out onto the beach, lays her eggs and goes back to the sea."

"Incredible, how many eggs does she lay?"

"About 120, which will produce about 70 to 80 young. But, quiet! They're coming!"

"Look, she's nervous. Since when do turtles breathe air?"

"They're cold-blooded reptiles over 180 million years old. Look, she's laying her eggs!"

"What do the young do when they're born?"

"After sixty days, they hatch at late afternoon and make for the sea, where there is more light. But there are a lot of predators on the way. That's why they're in danger of extinction."

"Isn't there anything we can do?"

"**Xcaret** Park has been working for turtle conservation for over three decades"

"How?"

"Through "Flora, Fauna y Cultura de México, A.C.", which is the environmental and cultural arm of **Xcaret**."

"We have to look after them!"

"Even more so in our country, because out of eight species in the world, six nest in Mexico, and four in Quintana Roo: the loggerhead, the hawksbill, the white and sometimes the leatherback."

"And what beaches do they nest on?"

"All along the coast."

SAVE THE MARINE TURTLE

The whale shark

"It's a whale shark, the biggest fish in the world! It's also called a domino, or checkerboard shark."

"Because of the spots that look like dominoes or checkers?"

"Yes. Each whale shark has its own pattern. It seems to be an individual identification."

"What are you doing? Are you going to get in and swim with that thing?"

"But of course. Come with me. They move very slowly, so you can swim with them."

"What if it gets hungry?"

"Take it easy! They only eat plankton and small fish."

"What if it thinks I look like plankton?"

"Come on! Look, it's turning round!"

"They are beautiful! When do they show up?"

"Between May and September you can see them near the islands of *Holbox* and Contoy. Fortunately, a Whale Shark Biosphere Reserve was declared as a way to protect them (2009).

Holbox Island

"This is a fisherman's paradise, with white beaches, palm trees, and that emerald sea!"

"Don't say it so loud, or everyone will come here."

"And the birds, the iguanas, the mangroves, the flamingos and the white sand."

"It's 25 miles long by 1.5 wide, and it's joined to the peninsula by a sand bank, with channels that connect the sea with the Yalahau lagoon."

"And the sandy streets! The colorful houses!"

"This is the Mexican Caribbean! In these waters there are dolphins, manta rays, hawksbill turtles and whale sharks. Fortunately, *Holbox* is protected: it belongs to the Yum Balam Flora and Fauna Protection Area."

"¡Mmm Smells delicious...or maybe I'm hungry."

"It's the lobster pizza they're making."

"What does *Holbox* mean?"

"It means "black hole" in Maya."

Contoy Island

"Did you bring sunglasses, a cap, biodegradable sunblock, insect repellent, camera and binoculars?"

"What for? There's nothing to do here. Just as well we dived in that place where we saw the corals, and even pink snails."

"It's the *Ixlaché* reef, which marks the beginning of the Great Mesoamerican Reef System."

"Isn't there anyone here?"

"Didn't you know? Contoy is an uninhabited island, but it's so important that it's protected as a National Park. It's almost 5.6 miles long, covers about 568 acres, and is the most important marine bird sanctuary in the Mexican Caribbean. There are 152 species of birds recorded as living here.

Starting in winter, over 10,000 birds concentrate here, including frigates, cormorants, boobies, herons, pelicans and sea swallows."

"And in summer?"

"Three species of marine turtle come to lay their eggs: the loggerhead, the hawksbill and the white."

"It's also a habitat for birds, reptiles, crustaceans and fish."

"There are thousands of them!"

"Over 234 species feed here, including manta rays and whale sharks. Let's go up the observation tower to see the whole beauty of the island from the top."

"Me first! Me first!"

"Afterwards we can eat *Tikin Xic*, that's baked fish, and then we'll go to the Puerto Viejo lagoon, where the brown pelicans nest. That's the biggest pelican on the Mexican Atlantic coast."

"You don't say! And I thought there was nothing to do!"

Ecological reserves
Nature sanctuaries

"11,500 square miles of jungle!"
"That's what Quintana Roo has. That's why it's the most forested state in Mexico. And that's not to mention the turquoise sea, the white sand beaches and the coral reefs."
"It's an ecological state."
"So ecological that almost a quarter is protected for conservation."
"Which are the protected areas in Quintana Roo?"
"Come with me. I'll show you on this map."

YUCATÁN

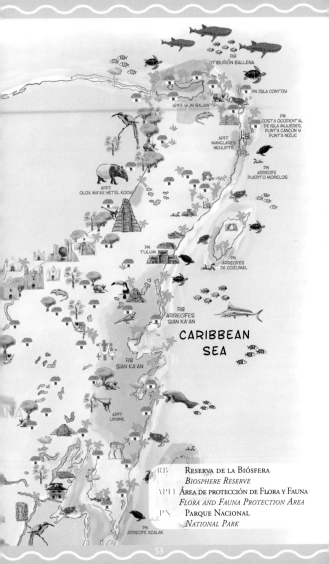

RB
TIBURÓN BALLENA

PN ISLA CONTOY

APFF YUM BALAM

PN
COSTA OCCIDENTAL
DE ISLA MUJERES,
PUNTA CANCÚN Y
PUNTA NIZUC

APFF
MANGLARES
NICHUPTÉ

PN
ARRECIFE
PUERTO MORELOS

APFF
OLOX MA'AX YETEL KOOH

PN
TULUM

PN
ARRECIFES
DE COZUMEL

RB
ARRECIFES
SIAN KA'AN

CARIBBEAN
SEA

RB
SIAN KA'AN

APFF
UAYMIL

RB   RESERVA DE LA BIÓSFERA
      Biosphere Reserve
APFF ÁREA DE PROTECCIÓN DE FLORA Y FAUNA
      Flora and Fauna Protection Area
PN   PARQUE NACIONAL
      National Park

PN
ARRECIFE XCALAK

53

Sian Ka'an Biosphere Reserve

"What does *Sian Ka'an* mean in Maya?"

""Place where the sky is born". It's a tropical jungle with flat land prone to flooding, and a wealth of vegetation and a diversity of ecosystems that favor the reproduction of a huge number of aquatic and land species."

"And no-one lives here?"

"Fortunately, it's difficult to get to this paradise. That's saved it from mass development plans."

"It's all beautiful!"

"The wetlands, lagoons and vegetation are so important for the ecology that in 1986 it was declared a Protected Area. And in 1987 the UNESCO designated it as a "World Heritage Site".

"It's a huge area!"

"It's about 2,500 square miles; the largest protected area on the Mexican Caribbean. In 1994 it was extended when the "Uaymil Flora and Fauna Protection Area" was established."

"Look, there are even places with archaeological remains."

"There are 23 known ones, some with ruins dating back 2300 years."

"Is this region that old?"

"*Sian Ka'an* is on a geological strip that's almost 2 million years old, the youngest in the country."

"I don't want to know what the oldest is!"

RESERVA DE
LA BIOSFERA
SIAN KA'AN

CARIBBEAN
SEA

Chinchorro Bank

"This is the largest coral atoll in America. It's a nature reserve covering 557 square miles."
"Vegetation, beaches and coral reefs!"
"It's two hours from the coast. These are incomparable places for diving and snorkeling."
"Plenty of ships must have been wrecked here."
"At least eighteen wrecks have been found from between 1600 and 1800. The Glenn View, a British cargo ship, sank here in 1960; the Ginger Scout, the Cassel, the Far Star, the Tropic, the Huba and the San Andrés all met the same fate."
"Hold on to me! I don't want to run aground on this atoll!"

GALLEON

GINGER SCOUT

PENELOPE

GLENN VIEW

19TH CENTURY GALLEON

CENTER KEY

KASSEL

TROPIC

XUBA

FAR STAR LOBOS KEY

Cozumel Reefs

"This is the Cozumel Reefs National Park!"
"I remember I saw it on television!"
"What did you see?"
"Jacques Cousteau, the French diver, do you remember? He showed Cozumel Reefs to the world."
"And so many people came that, to preserve it, the west coast of Cozumel Island had to be designated a Refuge Zone."
"It's almost completely surrounded by coral reefs."
"It's one of the most famous diving sites in the world!"
"How could it not be? The visibility is up to 200 feet. The water is between 79 and 82° F, and the beauty of the reef is unequaled in the world."
"Where do we get scuba equipment?"
"There's everything here for experts and novices. It's Cozumel!"

"Tell me, were the Ancient Maya here?"
"What a question! The oldest Mayan ruins
are around 3000 years old. In 350 AD, Cobá,
Kohunlich and *Dzibanché* were fully-fledged
cities. At their peak, in the Classical period
between 200 and 600 AD, they had a complex
system of social organization that is still
reflected in their urban centers."
"Where did the first settlements appear?"
"In the south, around 300 BC. The stone
buildings were constructed between 200 and
100 BC. At that time the Mayan cities in
Quintana Roo were so important that they
influenced the political and commercial life of

The pre-Hispanic period

Archaeological sites in Quintana Roo

the Petén region in Guatemala."

"You can see the size of these cities."

"*Dzibanché, Kohunlich, Ichkabal, Chakanbakán* and *Chacchoben* were large cities with acropolises, contemporary with *Calakmul* in Campeche; the kingdom of the snake head."

"*Calakmul*, is that the city with the masks?"

"The city that fell when Tikal rose to power in Guatemala. It expanded its influence over the cities of Quintana Roo, which reached their peak of development between the 7th and 9th centuries AD."

"And when did the Maya become maritime merchants?"

"After the collapse of the great Mayan kingdoms."
It was a time when the centers of power shifted to the Yucatan peninsula."
"Wasn't Tikal in control any more?"
"Those cities were abandoned, and gave way to cities like *Chichén Itzá* and *Tulum*, which reached their zenith in the Post-classical, and had Toltec features."
"Toltec?"
"Yes. A culture that flourished in the center of Mexico, and which exchanged cultural influences with the Maya. On the coast of Quintana Roo they commercialized salt."
"Salt?"
"Salt was a valued product at that time, and just so you know, the Maya were known throughout Mesoamerica as the Lords of Salt."
"Did these new cities last long?"
"They also collapsed, due to internal struggles, until the League of Mayapan was created, which unified territories and brought peace for two centuries. After that the smaller kingdoms and lordships formed."
"Was that what the Spanish found?"
"Yes, and they were able to use the political conflicts among the Maya of the time to their advantage."

Tulum

"What does *Tulum* mean?"
"In Maya it means wall, fence or enclosure, perhaps because of the wall surrounding the city."
"It seems to have been an important city."
"It was built around 800 to 900 AD, but reached its peak two centuries later under the rule of the *Itzaes*, when Mayapan fell. It was a major commercial port, where the rulers of Cobá and *Chichén Itzá* set sail with their merchandise for places as far away as Guatemala and Honduras."
"It's on a cliff facing the sea."
"That's the charm of *Tulum*. The city is the best example of East Coast style, which was dominant on the north coast of Quintana Roo in the Late Postclassical period (1400-1521 AD)."

TULUM!

"You certainly know your stuff!"
"Almost all the buildings at *Tulum* are low, with facades divided by moldings, flat roofs and walls that slope outwards. Walking through the streets of *Tulum*, surrounded by so much Mayan art, is an amazing experience."
"What did the Spanish think of it?"
"They were so impressed by the whole site that they considered it as big as Seville in Spain."
"Olé!"
"The Castle is the most outstanding building, because of its size, but there are others, like the Temple of Frescoes, the Temple of the Descending God and the Temple of the Wind; not to mention the residential buildings, like the House of Columns and the Palace of the *Halach Uinic*."

The Castle

"They say the Castle was used as a lighthouse for the vessels of Mayan merchants."

"It's impressive. Did you see the huge staircase?"

"It's flanked by balustrades and leads up to the upper temple, the one with the three entrances with columns like snakes. See it?"

"I can see there's an image above the central one."

"That's the Descending God, who was worshipped here."

"And what's that platform in front of the Castle?"

"It seems to have been for dancers. Other buildings in this complex are the Temple of the Initial Series and the Temple of the Descending God."

The temple of the Initial Series

"Why is this little temple so important?"
"Because it was near here that they discovered the Mayan stele with the earliest recorded date at Tulum: 564 AD."

Temple of the Descending God

"This is one of the most important buildings at Tulum, because of the bas-relief of the Descending God over the door."
"What does it represent?"
"Some say it symbolizes the setting sun, rain, or lightning. Others say it's the Bee God, *Ah Mucen Cab*. And yet others think it represents Venus entering the Underworld."

The Palace (House of the *Halach Uinic*)

"And these? They look like residential houses."
"The house of Columns is an example of residential architecture at Tulum. The same as the Palace, or House of the *Halach Uinic* (Great Lord in Maya), which has a remarkable niche with the figure of the Descending God."

Temple of the Wind God

"This is the Temple of the Wind God, it's connected to *Kukulcán*."
"It's not as if it's that windy."
"Look, "Hurricane" is a Mayan word."

I THINK WE OVERDID THE PRAYERS TO KUKULCÁN.

Temple of the Frescoes

SEE TULUM

"This is the most interesting building at *Tulum*. At first it was a room with a little altar against the wall."

"And those huge columns?"

"They were built later, as were the decorated frieze in both corners, with bas-reliefs of the God *Itzamná*."

"And why the frescoes?"

"Because of the Mayan paintings."

"Look: there are gods, snakes, marine motifs and offerings."

"It's Post-classical style, and shows the influence that art from the highlands of Mexico had on Mayan culture at this time."

NOT THAT, IDIOT! IT'S THE SAUCE!

Cobá

"What does Cobá mean?"

""Murky water". It's connected to the five lakes in the area, which made it one of the most powerful city-states in Mayan civilization."

"The most powerful?"

"Its history starts in the years 100-200 AD, but it reached its peak between 250 and 1000 AD. If I tell you it had 60,000 inhabitants, and links to the great Mayan city of Tikal."

"And when did it fall?"

"Between 1000 and 1200 AD, when *Tulum* and *Chichén Itzá* arose."

"Look at that huge pyramid!"

"That's the *Nohoch Mul*. With the Church and the Ball Court, it's one of the most important buildings at *Cobá*."

YOUR PUNISHMENT IS TO CARRY ME TO THE TOP OF THE PYRAMID!

Nohoch Mul

"It means "Large Mound". At 138 feet, it's one of the tallest buildings in the Mayan region."

"It's a symbol of power."

"It has seven levels and rounded corners, in an archaeological style more reminiscent of Tikal than the Mayan cities in Yucatan."

The Church

"This temple is high as well."

"It's almost 82 feet tall, and it's surrounded by palaces and residences."

"Ah, it's a building for the crème de la crème. The princesses of *Cobá* married the princes of Tikal."

The Ball Court

"And those figures on the panels of the Ball Court?"

"They depict prisoners and human skulls."

Chacchoben

"What are you doing up there?"

"I'm going to put an incense burner on the altar!"

"But that building's not used as a temple any more!"

"They told me that they've found a lot of incense burners from the time of the Ancient Maya."

"This place is impressive."

"*Chacchoben, Dzibanché, Kohunlich, Ichkabal* and *Chakanbakán* were influenced by the Mayan Petén region, whose principal city was *Tikal*."

"What does *Chacchoben* mean?"

""Place of colored corn". Corn made a city prosperous. It's believed that it was inhabited over two thousand years ago. The main buildings were constructed in the Classical period. It was at its height in the Early Classical (250-600 AD), and was abandoned around 700 AD."

"Look at those pyramids. It was an important city."

"The architecture of *Chacchoben* resembles that of the Petén more than the styles used in the north of Yucatan. Its nucleus covers around 173 acres of building complexes, the most important of which are The Great Base, the Roads, and Group II, which has the tallest building at the site. All the buildings show signs of different stages of construction, which is evidence for long occupation at the site."

"Everything looks so big!"

"The most significant building is the Great Base, which must have been the setting for religious ceremonies. Its Temple I seems to have been a register of calendar dates associated with the equinoxes and solstices, to indicate agricultural seasons."

"And the buildings along this really long street?"

"It's called The Roads, a complex of what must have been residences for the ruling class."

"*Chacchoben* has left me speechless."

CHACCHOBEN MAYA INCREASING THE GROSS DOMESTIC PRODUCT

Dzibanché

"Woww! What a huge city."
"At over 15 square miles, it was one of the largest in southern Quintana Roo. *Dzibanché* means "writing on wood," and refers to the beautiful wooden lintel 3, which still exists in Building VI."
"When was the city founded?"
"Around 200 BC, like almost all Mayan cities in the south of Quintana Roo. In its glory days it was so powerful that it competed with the great *Calakmul*, in the state of Campeche."
"I can see three architectonic groups."
"Each one with a different function."
"Which one has been most explored?"

"The Main Group complex, where there are typical examples of the early Classical, like Temple VI or Temple of the Lintels, the *Xibalbá* Plaza, and Temple I or Temple of the Owl."

"The Owl?"

"It's called that because of one of the jars with a lid in the shape of an owl that was found in the grave of a high-ranking woman. There's also Temple II, or Temple of the Cormorants, where two masks made of green stone mosaic were found."

"Ah! Those examples of Mayan beauty."

"There's also Temple XIII or Temple of the Captives, and the *Kinichná* complex, which seems to have been a funerary complex with the graves of rulers."

"When did *Dzibanché* decline?"

"People started to abandon it at the end of the Late Classical. In the 15th and 16th centuries the inhabitants only came into the ruins to leave offerings for their ancestors."

GREAT LORD OF DZIBANCHÉ TAKING ADVANTAGE OF HIS PRIVILEGES

Kinichná

"We're here at *Kinichná!*"

"Kinich-what?"

"*Kinichná*, which means "House of the Sun". It was dependent on *Dzibanché*. From its architecture, we can tell how important the city was."

"Right. Only an important city could have a huge pyramid like that one."

"It's the most important structure, known as the Acropolis. It's a three-stage pyramid."

"It's imposing, and all symmetrical."

"The first level takes you to a couple of side temples, and the same with the second level."

"You see? The higher you go, the narrower the steps get."

"At the top are three temples in a triangle around a central space."

"I'm going up!"

"Then you'll be able to see the stucco friezes painted on the walls inside the temple."

"Really?"

"Of course! They're paintings connected to the sun. They also found offerings and burials with jade objects."

"Jade? These lords had plenty of cocoa beans!"

"Plenty of cocoa and plenty of corn: *Kinichná* was a vigorous city."

"And a spectacular place. Look at all the trees around it."

GREAT LORD OF KINICHNÁ RELAXING

Kohunlich

"You look mesmerized."

"What do you expect with these beautiful masks?"

"*Kohunlich* is a corruption of the English name, Cohune (palm) Ridge. It has a style of its own, although you can see the influence of Petén and Río Bec styles."

"It's also ecological. Look at how many birds, reptiles and mammals there are!"

"This city was inhabited from 500 BC to 1100 AD. Here they constructed the famous Building of Masks, decorated with eight masks, only five of which survive. Today they are symbols of Quintana Roo."

"Spread the word!"

"Most of the buildings were constructed between late Classical and the Early Postclassical, like the Building of the Stelae, the 27 Steps and the *Pix'an* Complex."

"When did it start to decline?"

"Development continued into the Early Postclassical (900 – 1250 AD). Then building stopped and the people started to disperse."

"And to think there was so much greatness here!"

"After the Spanish conquest, the area was almost completely uninhabited until the late 19th and early 20th centuries, when the logging and gum camps arrived."

Tankah

"I want you to see *Tankah*, the old Mayan ceremonial center."

"Look, you can see its pyramids and temples used to have houses and palaces."

"They were residences for the priestly class. They found mural paintings here."

"And that pyramid?"

"That's Structure 1, thirteen feet high. From the top you can see the Caribbean Sea."

El Rey

"El Rey is a major Mayan port from the Late Post-classical period (1400-1550)."
"But it was founded much earlier, wasn't it?"
"It was inhabited from the Pre-classical, in 300 BC, but in the Postclassical it strengthened its position as a seaport with trade, fish, salt, honey and incense."
"So many buildings! And why is it called El Rey?"
"It was given that name because they found part of a sculpture that shows a human face with a very ornate head-dress, fit for a king."

Muyil

"I thought seeing *Muyil* would be great, but arriving along the canal...It was amazing!"

"I want you to be amazed by the archaeological wealth of Quintana Roo."

"Tell me the story of *Muyil*."

"The city is inside the *Sian Ka'an* Biosphere Reserve. It was inhabited from the Late Pre-classical (300 BC – 250 AD)."

"So these buildings, what era are they from?"
"Construction of the major buildings began in the Classical period, between 250 and 800 AD, but the architectonic remains date back to the Early Postclassical (900 to 1250) and the Late Postclassical (1400-1550), when *Muyil* was part of the Peninsula's great coastal commercial network."
"And they built the canal to join the lagoon with the Caribbean Sea."
"The site is divided into sectors A and B."
"*Muyil* A and B? I feel as if I'm in a supermarket."
"Muyil A is extensive and has several architectonic groups, with pyramidal bases, plazas, temples, platforms, a network of walls and an internal *sacbé* 550 yards long. Muyil B is made up of a few low platforms, a civic-religious building and several walls."
"And that tremendous pyramid?"
"That's the most important structure at *Muyil*. It's 56 feet tall, and it's known as The Castle."
"Muyil has an air of mystery."
"If these stones could talk..."

CARAVAN OF TAMEMES (BEARERS) ARRIVING TO TRADE AT MUYIL

San Gervasio

CONQUISTADOR TAKING NOTES ON THE CULT OF IX CHEL

"You're looking a funny color. What's wrong?"

"I'm seasick. Could you ask the ferryman to let me off here?"

"Oh yes, so you can call a cab in the middle of the ocean!"

"I'm serious. I've even forgotten where we're going."

"To Cozumel, a Caribbean island and the sanctuary of *Ix Chel*, Mayan fertility goddess."

"We're here!"

"Let's go to the San Gervasio archaeological site."

"San who? What kind of name is that?"

"It's the most important site on Cozumel. We don't know the original name, so it was named after the owner of the ranch where the archaeological ruins were found. It was founded in the early Classical (300 AD), and flourished around 600 AD."

"Was it a trading town?"

"From the year 1000 AD, under the hegemony of *Chichén Itzá*, San Gervasio formed part of the trading network that made the former a great city. Most of the buildings you can see today were built after 1200 AD."

"How big the city must have been!"

"They are architectonic complexes joined by a network of *sacbés* or white roads."

"Look at that building decorated with hands."

"It's called Little Hands. In the complex of palaces and temples there are The Alamo, The Murals, The Palace, The Ossuary and The Pilasters."

"And this one?"

"It's the Bat Complex, the oldest and best preserved. This one here is the *Nohoch Nah* or Big House, a temple from the Postclassical with fragments of mural painting. There's also the *Ka'na Nah* or High House, and the *Chichán Nah* or Little House."

"And all of them in East Coast style, right?"

"The typical style of the region."

"I love walking along the sacbés… Shall we go?"

"Wait for me! I thought you were seasick!"

Xel-Há

CONQUISTADOR "FOUNDING" SALAMANCA DE XALÁ

"**Xel-Há** was a prosperous port in the kingdom of Cobá. It first developed between 100 and 600 AD, and then reappeared around 1200 AD, when its wall was built. Today it's the most beautiful natural aquarium in the world, at the mouth of several of Quintana Roo's major underground rivers."

"When did people first hear of **Xel-Há**?"

"In 1527, before it was abandoned, when the Spanish called it Salamanca de *Xalá*."

"Is that the **Xel-Há** ecological site?"

"No, it's the archaeological site that contains pre-Hispanic ceremonial and religious monuments such as the Birds Group, with frescoes of local birds; the Jaguar Group, where you can see the figure of a jaguar; and the Pier Group. This site is opposite **Xel-Há** Park."

"**Xcaret** is the Ancient Mayan port city of *Polé*, which was at its peak in the Late Postclassical. Today it's home to an important living sample of the culture, flora and fauna of the region and from elsewhere in Mexico."

"What did they trade here?"

"Everything. In its heyday Mayan canoes were arriving and departing with feathers, gold and jade ornaments, obsidian knives, honey, incense, dried fish, turtle eggs, shells, corn and salt."

"What was its relationship with Cozumel?"

"Ceremonial: this was the departure point for canoes of Maya sanctified in the cenote, on their way to the island sanctuary of *Ix Chel* (goddess of fertility, of the moon and of medicine, as well as inspiration for the Sacred Journey)."

"Imagine the faces of the Spanish when they came to **Xcaret**."

"They even built a Catholic chapel!"

ANCIENT MAYAN MERCHANDIZING

El Meco

"The name [mec in Mayan means pigeon-toed] comes from the nickname of a lame man who had a ranch on the site."

"And from when was it inhabited?"

"From 200 AD, as a fishing village. It was abandoned around 600 AD and reoccupied in 1000 AD first by the *Itzaes* from *Chichén Itzá* and later by the *Cocom* from Mayapán. El Meco was a prosperous commercial and religious port."

"Look at that pyramid. It's so high, and so well-preserved!"

"That's The Castle, it's 41 feet high, the tallest in northern Quintana Roo. That palace is Structure 12, the second most important at El Meco. It was used for political and administrative functions."

"What a wealth of archaeology there is in the

Oxtankah

"*Oxtankah* means "among breadnut trees"."

"What did you expect? It's full of breadnut trees."

"It was important for exporting salt."

"When did *Oxtankah* grow up?"

"The most important buildings were erected in the Early Classical (200-600 AD). In 600 AD it was abandoned, and then repopulated."

"A lot of the buildings are well-preserved."

"Here are the Plaza of the Bees, with its palace and altar in the center, and the Plaza of the Columns with its palace decorated with stuccoes."

"Look, that looks like a chapel!"

"It's the Spanish Chapel, built in the 16th or 17th century, it's the most recent structure at *Oxtankah*."

Chakanbakán

"This site is surrounded by the Om lagoon!"
"*Chakanbakán* means "surrounded by savannah".
It's an ecological reserve."
"How was *Chakanbakán* built?"
"To lay out the city and construct the buildings,
they cut and leveled the land."
"It must have been really complicated."
"Besides that, they considered it a strategic site
against enemy attacks and flooding."
"Is it very old?"
"The first inhabitants, who came from the Petén
in Guatemala, arrived around 300 BC, during
the Late Preclassical. The golden age was during
the Classical period (250 to 900 AD)."

"And until when was the city inhabited?"

"Until the Late Postclassical (1200-1545 AD). It was abandoned after the Spanish arrived."

"Look at that pyramid!"

"It's the Acropolis, the largest structure of its kind, over 650 feet along each side and more than 32 feet high. On top of it they built palaces, platforms, temples, a ball court and other structures."

"And that building?"

"That's Pyramid 1, the highest at the site. It's called *Nohoch Balam*. On the sides they found six huge masks made of stucco, mud and stone, with features that appeared at the same time Olmec and Maya. The largest measures ten feet high and 32 feet wide."

"The grandeur of our ancestors!"

ACCORDING TO THIS MAP YOU SHOULD HAVE FOUND KING PAKAL'S TOMB BY NOW.

The Colonial Era
Time of the Encomienda

"Mestizaje, the mixing of the races, started in Quintana Roo, you know."

"Tell me all about it!"

"It was when the Spaniard Gonzalo Guerrero was shipwrecked and rescued by the Maya, and married the princess *Zazil Ha*, daughter of the lord of Chactemal."

"Pure soap opera!"

"Not really. At that time, from the mid-16th century to part of the 19th, the peninsula was under the control of the Spanish Audiencia of Mexico."

"Quintana Roo as well?"

"Quintana Roo didn't exist as a State; the Peninsula was divided in five provinces: Campeche, Mérida, Valladolid, Bacalar and Tabasco. The political capital was in Mérida."

"And the Maya put up with it?"

"They were never completely conquered, but the religion gradually imposed itself to the extent that, from 1518, Cozumel was the seat of the Caroline Bishopric (so called in honor of the Emperor Charles V), the first diocese in Mexico."

"How come you know so much?"

"I'm in love with my homeland, my dear."

"Just with your homeland?"

"Talking of land, the colonial economy was based on rice, cocoa and fruit trees. Also cotton, salt and dyes such as indigo and logwood. There were sugar, cane alcohol, honey, incense and precious woods."

"As far as I can see, the Maya did all the work."

"With blood and sweat: the encomienda was an extremely harsh system."

"Encomienda?"

"Yes, an invention of the Spanish, in which they were given a group of natives, with land included, and the Indians paid tribute in kind and with work."

"And what did they get in exchange?"

"Education and evangelization."

"Not a good deal for the Maya, was it?"

"Terrible: the encomenderos ended up being owners of the land assigned to the natives."

"Are there any relics of that time?"

"There are surviving churches whose imposing size speaks of the importance of these places under the Colony."

"Can you visit them?"

"Of course! There's even an itinerary designed to see them, called "The Church route"."

The Church route

"How long ago did the first Spanish Catholics arrive in the peninsula?"

"They say around 1534. A quarter of a century later, they created the Franciscan Province of San José de Yucatán, which included what is now Quintana Roo. The first missionaries set about finding prosperous Mayan villages in order to establish their headquarters there."

"Headquarters?"

"Yes, the places their missions to evangelize the Maya would set out from."

"Where did they start?"

"In Tihosuco. That's why there was an uprising there. Suffice to say that in 1605 a large number of Maya, accused of idolatry, had fled to the islands of the Mexican Caribbean."

"And the evangelizers...Did they evangelize?"

"When you see the churches of the region you'll be able to answer that question yourself."

"This area's very nice."

"It's the south of the State."

"Very different from the north."

"Extremely. Here is the Mayan heart of Quintana Roo, beating in the middle of an exuberant jungle with lagoons, cenotes and many communities that keep the language and traditions of their ancestors alive."

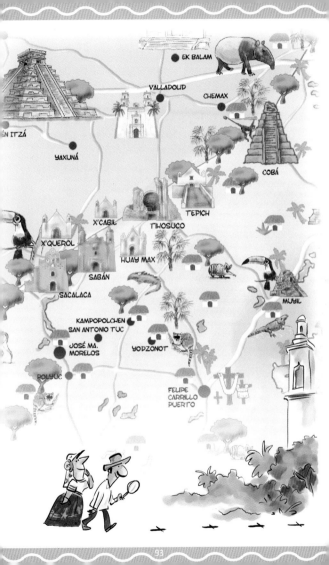

EK BALAM

VALLADOLID

CHEMAX

EN ITZÁ

YAXUNÁ

COBÁ

TEPICH

X'CABIL

TIHOSUCO

X'QUEROL

HUAY MAX

SABÁN

SACALACA

MUYIL

KAMPOPOLCHEN
SAN ANTONIO TUC

JOSÉ MA.
MORELOS

YODZONOT

POLYUC

FELIPE
CARRILLO
PUERTO

Felipe Carrillo Puerto

"I bet you can't say the real name of this place: *Noh Cah* Santa Cruz *Balam Nah Kampokolche.*"

"Good heavens!"

"It was founded with that name on the 15th October 1850, but it was called *Chan* Santa Cruz or Little Santa Cruz. In 1932 it was rebaptized with the name Felipe Carrillo Puerto."

"The socialist governor of Yucatan. And that church?"

"It's the old *Balam Nah* church, which seems to be the only one in America built by the natives. In 1854 the rebel Maya erected it in just nine months. It's 39 feet high, 39 feet wide 98 feet long, with walls five feet thick. By the way, the cross isn't the original."

"It's an impressive church!"

Sacalaca

"Is it true there are two churches here?"

"Yes. One for whites and one for Indians."

"Are they both old?"

"The older is the one for whites, consecrated to the Virgin Mary. It's in the center of Sacalaca."

"Is it that one? But...it's beautiful!"

"It was an open chapel which over time was decorated with that spandrel of three belfries. They put sculptures in the niches and carved stone cornices and pilasters. The walls had embedded figures of Adam and Eve."

"And the other church is the one in the Indian quarter?"

"Yes. It was built without decoration. The crown-shaped spandrel functioned as a belfry. You can still see the original colors."

"I've really enjoyed getting to know Sacalaca."

X'querol

"What does *X'querol* mean in Maya?"

""Place of the fresh corn drink". It's a small community on the border with the State of Yucatan."

"Is that the church?"

"It was never finished, because of the Caste War. The locals say that when they arrived, the church had been covered by underbrush. It seems that's what preserved it."

"It looks very nicely done up."

"It's been restored, so we can appreciate the smooth, white facade with no niches or windows, and the stone cross at the top."

"And those little towers at the sides?"

"They're stone needles, and each one has a small bell. It's the classic chapel structure with a bower roof."

Sabán

"Why is the church at *Sabán* so huge?"

"Because of its importance under the Colony. When it was built in 1795, there were 2,259 inhabitants."

"It must have taken a lot of building material."

"This Franciscan church is the second largest on the Route. Imagine the size of the Mayan temple that was here before!"

"Look at the Baroque columns at the entrance!"

"And the carved image of St. Peter up there with the Rooster of the Passion, not to mention the towers and the spandrel. It was never finished: during the Caste War, *Sabán* changed hands several times, between the Maya and the government forces."

"What's inside the church?"

"A plaque with the image of St. Peter."

Huay Max

"What does *Huay Max* mean?"

"In Maya it means "he who is a sorcerer." The church is another victim of the Caste War."

"Why do you say that?"

"See the choir ceiling? There are burnt beams and at the sides you can see where the altars were sacked."

"But everything's very clean?"

"The locals recently did it up as it always was: a place of worship."

"The bell-tower is very pretty."

"It has spandrels with triple bell towers and a smooth facade with a triangular top in the center."

"It's a charming little church."

X'cabil

"This much is certain: the Maya produced honey here."

"They were experts, my dear, and some of it remains, because here there are guilds in honor of the Virgin, and festivals in honor of the god of rain."

"Look at the church; it's on a little hill."

"It's a modest church, typical of the region."

"It's very well-preserved."

"Take a photo, would you? We're leaving for *Tihosuco*."

"Tihuwhat?"

Tihosuco

"Tihosuco, from the Maya Jo'o, five, and Tssuk, stomach; it was the capital of the lordship of Cochuah, and was conquered by Francisco de Montejo in 1544."

"What a great Franciscan church!"

"The friars chose Tihosuco as their headquarters from which to evangelize the center of the peninsula. Over the years it filled with Spanish and mestizo families."

"That's why these colonial houses are so beautiful."

"Tihosuco was so prosperous that it attracted pirates."

"Pirates? But we're a long way from the sea!"

"In 1686, Laurens de Graaf and Michel de Grammont, on their way to Valladolid, sacked Tihosuco."

"Were they the ones who left the church and monastery half-ruined?"

"Only the walls are left of the monastery, and it's now a cemetery. The church (dedicated to the Holy Infant Jesus) was finished in 1839."

"Was there war here?"

"The Caste War, but I'll tell you about that later."

Tepich

"Who's the character with the machete in this statue?"

"Read what it says."

""Glory to Cecilio Chí! Liberator of the Mayan nation and immortal symbol of justice and liberty!""

"Cecilio Chí was born here. He started the Caste War on July 30´1847, when he raised up the Maya against the Spanish landowners, with the aim of obtaining their freedom. That's why Tepich is known as the cradle of the Caste War."

"Ahh! That's why the anthem says: "In Tepich the courage of the Maya, Turned oppression into victory..."

"Did you see the church? It was built on the ruins of an ancient Mayan temple. It had a straw roof and a sober design, with lateral towers and a triangular facade."

"What's that next to the church?"

"It's the tomb where the hero of Tepich, Cecilio Chí, is buried."

"Why were there so many pirates in Quintana Roo?"
"Pirates and buccaneers saw this thinly populated area as the ideal lair to hide their ill-gotten booty. Henry Morgan even repaired his damaged ships on Cozumel."
"Morgan...and did other famous pirates come here?"
"Some terrible ones! Abraham; "Diego the Mulatto"; "Peg-Leg" (Cornelis Jol), Laurens de Graaf, the Lafitte brothers; Grammont, and the Scot Peter Wallace, who came to transform the political geography of the region with the trade in logwood."
"They were traders?"
"Smugglers, because it was more lucrative than

Pirates in Quintana Roo

piracy. In the mid-18th century, the pirates were involved in smuggling precious woods and European products that they brought into Ascension Bay and Bacalar. Contraband was the key to the flowering of Bacalar and other villages like Telá, *Sabán* and *Tihosuco*."

"How long did this go on?"

"Until 1763, when thanks to an agreement between Spain and England, the English were granted the right to stay in the lands of Belize in order to exploit logwood. Then everything changed in the 19th century, with added elements which were decisive factors during the Caste War."

The Island of Cozumel

"The first pirate attack was here?"

"In 1571 the pirate Pierre de Sanfroy, who had just attacked Hunucmá in Yucatán, and was being pursued by the Spanish, went into hiding in the church of St. Clement in Boca Iglesia, near Cabo Catoche."

"He stopped to pray?"

"Far from it! He went through **Xcaret** and sacked the island of Cozumel, defiling the little church of St. Michael, using the altar as a bed and the sacristy as a toilet."

"Jesus, Mary and Joseph!"

"But the Spanish were hard on his heels, so Sanfroy fled with his pirates to Santa María *Oxkib* (perhaps what is now El Cedral, another village on Cozumel), and there they caught him."

"Finally!"

"Four of them were executed in Merida; another six, including Sanfroy, were tried in Mexico City by the Inquisition. But don't think they were tried as pirates."

"As what, then?"

"As Huguenots, in other words, as Protestants, so I'm sure they made it hot for them!"

"And did more pirates come?"

"No-one knows how many came this way, but it's certain that they came. We know that in 1713 four English pirate ships came to sack, burn and kidnap the inhabitants, turning Cozumel into a den for their barbarities. And like Morgan, the Dutch pirate Jean Lafitte also repaired his ships here."

"Didn't they ever stay to live here?"

"Never! There was no one to feed them here. On the other hand, there were long occupations while they cut the logwood that brought them so much profit."

THE PIRATE SANFROY AND HIS BANDITS DEFILING THE CHURCH OF ST. MICHAEL ON THE ISLAND OF COZUMEL.

Bacalar

"Between 415 and 435 AD, the Itzaes founded *Siyan Ka'an Bakhalal*, as a key point for trade with Central America."

"What did they trade?"

"Quetzal feathers, cotton blankets and salt. In 1531, the conquistador Alonso Dávila founded the village of Villa Real, which didn't last a minute, because the Maya continually attacked it."

"But the Spanish were already in Bacalar."

"In 1543, Gaspar Pacheco and his son Melchor defeated the Maya. Melchor founded Bacalar, with the name Salamanca de Bacalar."

"So? Do you want me to applaud?"

"In 1630 it was the last Spanish bastion in the region, with only 28 inhabitants, but it was still the supply post en route to Guatemala and Honduras."

"When did the pirates arrive?"

"Throughout the 17th century, pirates arrived by land or by sailing up the Río Hondo, and attacked Bacalar. Sometimes with extreme ferocity, like the attack of "Diego the Mulatto" in 1652, or that of the pirate Abraham, who sacked it twice and left it destroyed and almost abandoned."

"So what did the Spanish do?"

"They sent expeditions looking for their lairs along the coast of Belize, but it wasn't much use."

"Why not?"

"In 1727, pirates from Belize disembarked in Ascension Bay and got as far as *Tihosuco*."

"That's right! You told me that."

"Marshal Antonio de Figueroa y Silva ordered the construction of the San Felipe de Bacalar Fort. So Bacalar was repopulated and prospered exporting mahogany, logwood, sugar, some fruit, goats and pigs."

"This bastion of Quintana Roo was built in 1733."

"No pirate's coming near a fort like that."

"But they did. English colonists attacked it between 1751 and 1754, and in 1798 it was vital to the Spanish efforts when they decided to expel the English from Belize. In 1847, its 250 soldiers and 5063 inhabitants experienced the horrors of the Caste War. The Mayan rebels held the fort for almost half a century, until the end of the war in 1901, when they gave it up without a shot being fired."

"And who achieved that feat?"

"Othón P. Blanco, the man who founded Payo Obispo."

"Which today is Chetumal!"

"The fortress had 24 cannon divided among four bulwarks and a central observation tower which housed a chapel, powder store, quarters for the troops and a weapons room."

"And this ditch? It runs right round the fort."

"It was widened, so they had to build a drawbridge to get in."

Fort San Felipe Museum

"This museum is fantastic! It has background music and video screens."

"Yes, here they recreate the pirate attacks."

"Did you see? In the first room there are pieces rescued from the lagoon and collections of pre-Hispanic and colonial objects...There are replicas of ships. Look at that mural!"

"It's called "Defense of Fort San Felipe Bacalar", by Elio Carmichael. It shows the natives' struggle to defend the fort during the Caste War."

"It's a lovely museum."

Isla Mujeres

"Why is it called Isla Mujeres (Island of Women)?"
"Because when the Spanish arrived in 1517, they found female figures which the Maya offered to *Ix Chel*, the goddess of fertility."
"And this hacienda? It has a pirate shield!"
"It's the Mundaca hacienda, which Fermín Antonio de Mundaca y Maréchega built in 1860. He was a pirate and slaver who settled here because they gave him well-water to drink."
"Well-water?"
"La Trigueña, a native woman with hair the color of corn, captivated him to such an extent that Mundaca, who had faced the British Navy, left his wanderings to build this hacienda here with arches and gardens and an orchard, so that he and la Trigueña could write a love story which is now part of the islanders' cultural tradition."
"Give me a hug, dear, I'm so moved!"
"Because of this story, Isla Mujeres is the ideal place for newly-weds."
"That doesn't suggest anything to you, dear?"
"Wouldn't you rather go diving?"
"With you! You and I alone together on this famous island."
"It became famous when the Mexican oceanographer Ramón Bravo showed the world the "Cave of Sleeping Sharks"."
"Come over here, honey, let's not wake them up."

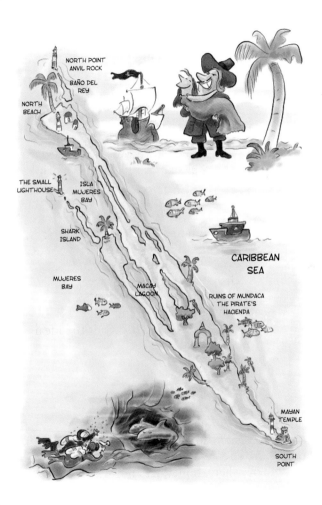

NORTH POINT
ANVIL ROCK

BAÑO DEL
REY

NORTH
BEACH

THE SMALL
LIGHTHOUSE

ISLA
MUJERES
BAY

SHARK
ISLAND

MUJERES
BAY

MACAY
LAGOON

CARIBBEAN
SEA

RUINS OF MUNDACA
THE PIRATE'S
HACIENDA

MAYAN
TEMPLE

SOUTH
POINT

MUSA
Subacuatic Art Museum

"I don't want to jump in!"

"You'll be fine!"

"That's what you say. From here all I can see are people who I'm sure heard the same as you told me, and there they are, all petrified at the bottom of the sea."

"They're sculptures, dear. So, last one in's a rotten egg!"

"Glug glug!...I can talk...Can you hear me?"

"Of course I can hear you. Look around."

"I don't believe it. It's so beautiful!"

"We're in the largest underwater museum in the world, at the bottom of the sea in the Isla Mujeres West Coast, Punta Cancun, Punta Nizuc National Park."

"Who made all these life-size sculptures? It's absolutely incredible!"

"Jason de Caires Taylor is the artist. He's a sculptor, and he made over 400 pieces to set up the underwater space you can see in front of you. The idea is to create a medium where art and nature can co-exist."

"The sculptures are full of coral! Look at that woman lying back and meditating!"

"The sculptures aren't static: they continue the creation process in a natural way. That woman is the gardener; the corals have established themselves on her, creating new forms on the same sculpture. The same thing happens with the other pieces."

"This museum is unique!"

"It's not finished yet, but it's been visited by divers from all over the world."

The Caste War

"So, now tell me. What is the war and what were the castes?"

"It's a misnomer, because there were no castes here; what we know as the "Caste War" was an uprising of native Maya against the white and mestizo population."

"And when was that?"

"It broke out in Tepich on the 30th July 1847, and it ended in 1901. The Maya had often risen up in arms against oppression. The first time was in 1546, against the encomiendas in Valladolid and Bacalar."

"They must have been very badly treated."

"There were a lot of revolts between 1639 and 1655, before the uprising against the Spanish led by Jacinto *Canek* in 1761. That was the direct precursor of the Caste War."

"It seems to have been a bloody war."
"I'd better not go into detail, but you ought to
know that the Maya came very close to winning
the war: in May 1848 the white population
was on the point of being expelled from the
Peninsula, but the rains came and the Indians
went back to their lands."
"They lost because of the rain?"
"Well, they had to sow crops."
"And then?"
"Nothing. The government forces counter-
attacked and recovered several villages."
"What did the Maya do?"
"They went into the jungle, and supported by
the English in Belize (British Honduras), they
held out against the Mexican army until 1901."

Chan Santa Cruz

"We've been here!"

"I'm going to tell you the whole story: in 1850 the Maya were defeated, but they got a second chance when the "Talking Cross" appeared."

"A talking cross?"

"In mid-1850, José María Barrera, a mestizo deserter, discovered a spring near Kampocolché. To mark its location he carved three crosses on the bark of a mahogany tree."

"That was the Talking Cross?"

"The Maya took it as a miracle, and brought offerings. Around the crosses they founded the village of *Chan* Santa Cruz (Little Holy Cross)."

"When did the cross start to speak?"

"Barrera had three wooden crosses made, and convinced the people that they had fallen from heaven to support the rebellion."

"Did they believe him?"

"He became the patron of the Talking Cross, the person who received messages from God. A ventriloquist, Manuel Nahuat, revealed the messages."

"What did the messages say?"

"That they had to keep fighting against the whites. Barrera built a temple. The Talking Cross was kept in a room called "The Holy Glory". There the Mayan priests met to celebrate sacred rituals inherited from their ancestors."

"Was *Chan* Santa Cruz taken by the army?"

"It upheld the revolt, with an economy that

allowed it to buy guns from the English in Belize."

"The crosses worked."

"When the border conflict with Belize was resolved, *Chan* Santa Cruz was taken on the 3rd of May 1901 by General Ignacio A. Bravo. He started colonization with the exploitation of precious woods and logwood."

"Did the Maya never come back?"

"In 1915, Salvador Alvarado returned *Chan* Santa Cruz to them, but he transferred the capital to Payo Obispo - now Chetumal. This depopulated the Mayan village, which was repopulated later thanks to Francisco *May*, a character who monopolized the production of gum, the main export at the time."

"When did *Chan* Santa Cruz change its name?"

"In 1932. It was named after the great Yucatecan leader Felipe Carrillo Puerto."

"It's a place full of history!"

"And we haven't seen the Caste War Museum yet."

Caste War Museum

"Open your eyes!"

"*Tihosuco*!"

"Now you know so much about the Maya's struggles, I want you to see the Caste War Museum in *Tihosuco*, a historic treasure in the Mayan heart of Quintana Roo."

"This building is colonial."

"It was the house of a 17th-century hacienda owner, although there are those who say that Jacinto *Pat* himself lived here."

"Jacinto *Pat*?"

"One of the Mayan leaders who started the Caste War, along with Cecilio *Chí* and Manuel Antonio *Ay*."

"When was this museum opened?"

"In 1993, and it has four rooms. Come on, let's go in the first."

"Look, there are photographs, models and documents."

"Everything is connected to the native movement against the Spanish. Did you see the second room? Here you can see what life was like in the peninsula in the 19th century, after Independence."

"The third room has objects they used to use then!"

"And papers which explain the causes of the Caste War. In the fourth room there are weapons, models and documents that recount the development of this Mayan social war, and the founding of *Chan* Santa Cruz. It's an extraordinary museum that also showcases the pictorial work of Marcelo Jiménez."

"Now I understand the Yucatan peninsula's Caste War!"

"And this museum is the legacy of that Mayan rebellion."

Chewing gum and logwood

"Since when has there been chewing gum in Quintana Roo?"

"The ancient Maya used to extract gum latex (*sicté*) from the sapodilla tree (*yaa*) and they used it for chewing, as an adhesive, and to light incense."

"When did the chewing gum industry begin?"

"Starting in the mid-19th century several companies were set up here to exploit logwood, and then moved on to gum, tobacco, vanilla and precious woods like cedar, mahogany and guayacán."

"Were they Mexican companies?"

"Concessions were granted to companies that became the largest landowner in Mexico. One of them was managed by the Compañía Agrícola, founded by a millionaire sisal grower, who operated with Mexican and Cuban labor. The Compañía Colonizadora de la Costa Oriental de Yucatán was established in Santa María Colony,

which is now Leona Vicario."

"Why is chewing gum so closely linked to North American culture?"

"Chewing gum as it is known worldwide was invented by a New York family called Adams, who were friendly with the exiled ex-president of Mexico Antonio López de Santa Anna. He introduced them to gum. After several experiments with sugar and flavorings, they invented the famous Adams Chewing Gum."

"And Mexican chewing gum...for export."

"So much that you can find vestiges of gum tappers' camps on the route of the rail trucks from Santa María to Punta Corcho, where they built head offices and camps such as Rémula, La Tuxpeña, Santa Matilde and Central Vallarta, which was a gum camp in the early 20th century."

Leona Vicario
Ex-hacienda Santa María

"Is it true that there used to be a colony here?"

"The Santa María Colony, founded in 1896 by the Compañía Colonizadora de la Costa Oriental de Yucatán, the principal gum tappers' camp in the north of Quintana Roo. It was a concession from the federal government to the "Banco de Londres y Mexico" for the exploitation of gum and logwood."

"Where did the people who settled here come from?"

"From all over, especially from Tuxpan, Veracruz. But it wasn't easy: the climate, disease and many Maya still in arms who attacked the gum camps."

"Were there other tappers' villages nearby?"

"Leona Vicario was linked to other villages by rail tracks with trucks pulled by mules.

GUM TRUCK ARRIVING AT THE SANTA MARIA HACIENDA.

The circuit linked Chiquilá, Kantunilkín, Leona Vicario and Central Vallarta with Puerto Morelos, the port for shipping to the United States, Europe and Asia."

"When was the gum season?"

"From September to February. Six months of hard work. For the other six, they survived in the jungle."

"The people were unemployed?"

"Yes. That brought alcohol and gambling. Death and duels were commonplace."

"When did it change its name?"

"With the agrarian policies of president Lázaro Cárdenas the Santa Maria Colony was transferred to the federal government and several villages were created. Since the state bore the illustrious name of Andrés Quintana, they chose the name of his wife, Leona Vicario, for Santa Maria, and this became official on the 7th of March 1936."

Puerto Morelos

"How old is Puerto Morelos?"
"We know there were settlements of Mayan sailors here, but the modern history of the place starts in 1898, with the famous Compañía Colonizadora de la Costa Oriental de Yucatán."
"I know, the one that exploited logwood, tobacco, vanilla, cedar and gum, among other things."
"Exactly. When it was known as Punta Corcho, the wood was thrown into the sea to be picked

up by small boats and loaded onto the ships that would take it abroad."

"Wasn't there a wharf?"

"No. Some time later the "Banco de Londres y México" built warehouses and the first wooden wharf, when they were granted the concession for exploiting gum and created the "Colonia Santa María" company."

"And Puerto Morelos was born, exit port for chewing gum!"

"Yes. Around 1929, Puerto Morelos already had wooden houses, a wharf, a main street and a store. There was an air of prosperity until 1934 and the post-war collapse of the industry."

"What happened to the village?"

"It wasn't until the 1970s, when the opening of Cancun provided a new phase of economic growth for the town. People from other parts of the country and abroad came to the port, initiating a new economic colonization.""

Modern times

THREE CHEERS FOR QUINTANA ROO!

"On the 24th of November 1902, the Territory of Quintana Roo was created by presidential decree."

"With the full force of law?"

"In February 1904 the new Law for the Political and Municipal Organization of the Territory of Quintana Roo was issued. It fixed the boundaries and defined political functions."

"But that was the time of the Revolution!"

"That's why, in 1913, Venustiano Carranza made Quintana Roo part of Yucatan again. But on the 26th of June 1915 he restored the Territory of Quintana Roo."

"He changed his mind. Wasn't that the year that *Chan* Santa Cruz was handed over?"

"That was a few days earlier, between the 14th and 18th of June, when the Maya were given back their sacred city and troops were sent to Payo Obispo, which would later become the capital of the Territory."

"That changed the history of the State."
"Of course. *Chan* Santa Cruz was deserted.
It took four years to repopulate it, under the
leadership of the native General Francisco May."
"The one Carranza named Constitutionalist
General?"
"He recognized him as leader of all the Maya
and granted him permission to exploit – tax-free
– 77 square miles of jungle."
"The general amassed quite some power!"
"He monopolized the buying and selling of
gum, and concentrated so much political
power that *Chan* Santa Cruz was, in practice,
independent of the rest of Quintana Roo and
the country."
"When did he lose these privileges?"
"With the world crisis of 1929. May lost power
and the federal government sent the 36th Battalion.

That's how the federal government came into the area."

"Was that good or bad?"

"Depends. Rumors began to spread that the Territory ought to disappear."

"No. Again?"

"And it happened again: on the 14th of December 1931, President Pascual Ortíz Rubio decreed the annexation of Quintana Roo to Yucatán and Campeche."

"And why was that, I'd like to know?"

"Because, they said, it meant an enormous expense for the country, although that wasn't true."

"And how did they get the Territory back?"

"I'm not going to go into the huge problems they had with depopulation, taxes and even confrontations. What I will say is that there was such a persistent campaign that, on the 11th of January 1935, President Lázaro Cárdenas decreed the creation (again) of the Federal Territory of Quintana Roo, with its old borders and extension."

"What a struggle! And was that the last time?"

"The last. From then on Quintana Roo's economic rise began."

"And we're into the 1940s!"

"They were years of prosperity. The Second World War favored chewing gum production and it reached the highest levels in its history."

"Everything was plain sailing?"

"Until the 28th of September 1955, when Hurricane Janet hit the south of Quintana Roo, leaving many people dead or missing."

"That's terrible!"

"This was the time of Margarito Ramírez, a very controversial governor who kept himself in power for 14 years of government so corrupt that there were forceful demonstrations that ended in his destitution on the 15th of January 1959."

"Nothing lasts forever."

"In the 1960s there were great changes, propitiated by President López Mateos. Infrastructure and roads were built. Everything to convert the Territory into a free and sovereign State. Not so much chewing gum was being produced, but there were new projects for the area."

"Tourism!"

"Cancun was developed. It was the first time a policy of promoting tourism had been elaborated."

"And was Quintana Roo a State yet?"

"On the 8th of October 1974, Quintana Roo was born as a free and sovereign State!"

"Three cheers for Quintana Roo!"

"That's right, for the place where the sun is born, for its beauty and its welcoming people, which have made it a tourist attraction par excellence."

"Let the facts speak for themselves!"

Chetumal

"This is the cradle of mestizaje, because the first mixing of races in America happened here, when the shipwrecked sailor Gonzalo Guerrero became so assimilated into Mayan life that he ended up marrying the daughter of the chief, with whom he had several children."

"He's even mentioned in the anthem!"

"And the city is linked to the Caste War. Since the rebels were acquiring their weapons in Belize, a military post was set up on the border. In 1898, Lieutenant Othón Pompeyo Blanco founded Payo Obispo. It was a hamlet that in 1936 would be named Chetumal, from Chac-Temal, the Mayan village on the site."

"And the village grew, didn't it?"

"It was a town of wooden houses, which was devastated by Hurricane Janet in 1955. It was rebuilt and declared capital of the State of Quintana Roo."

"How was it populated?"

"Duty-free trade attracted immigrants who made Chetumal a place where the descendants of Maya mixed with mulattos from Belize, mestizos and foreigners from different countries."

Cancún

"And to think this used to be a desert island!"
"And in the most abandoned spot in the Caribbean."
"How did it become a tourist destination?"
"You only have to look at this turquoise sea, that white sand, these palm trees..."
"It's paradise!"
"During the 1970s, the importance of tourism led the government to construct tourist cities from scratch. Cancun was one of them."
"It was certainly worthwhile."
"Today it welcomes several million tourists a year, and it's the most important tourist destination in Mexico and the world."
"Of course it is! Its closeness to archaeological sites makes it an entranceway to the Mayan World, and the top tourist destination in the Caribbean. In foreign exchange it generates more than a third of the country's tourist income."

Playa del Carmen

"In the beginning this used to be a fishing village where you caught the ferry to Cozumel Island."

"There's nothing village about it now."

"In the 1980s and 90s, European tourists found a village with few services, and opened their own businesses, so now there are European style hotels and hostels, and restaurants serving fine French and Italian cuisine."

"Look, it's Fifth Avenue, with its stores and open-air cafés!"

"The city is between *Tulúm* and Cancun, an hour from Cobá and very close to beaches, cenotes and ecological parks. That makes it the ideal starting point for a tour of Quintana Roo."

Cozumel Island

"It's the largest inhabited island in Mexico."

"I already know it was a ceremonial center for the Maya, that it had pirates, that chewing gum and logwood were shipped from here, and that colonists who came here were escaping the Caste War."

"It became known worldwide in the 1960s, and today it's one of the best sites for recreational diving, and an important point on Caribbean cruise routes."

"And this museum?"

"It's the Cozumel Island Museum, a quick look at the history of the island, from its formation to its role as a modern tourist destination."

"Look at this coral!"

"These are exhibitions of the features of coral reefs and the island's ecosystems."

The Mayan Riviera

"What is this about a Mayan Riviera?"

"Between 1250 and 1550 AD, the area that we know today as the Mayan Riviera was a commercial and religious region for the Ancient Maya. Cities arose, such as **Tulum**, the port of *Polé* (now **Xcaret**) and **Xel-Há**."

"There was a lot of activity in the area!"

"When the Spanish arrived in the 16th century it was abandoned for the next three centuries."

"Well it's obviously made a comeback!"

"Today it's a coastal tourist region 81 miles long, from Puerto Morelos to Punta Allen, parallel to the Great Mesoamerican Reef. It has underground rivers, cenotes and jungle surrounding beaches and villages, full of exotic animals and archaeological remains that guard the secrets of the enigmatic Mayan civilization."

The Mayan Coast

"After the Riviera we have the Mayan Coast. This is 62 miles of beaches, mangroves and palm trees stretching from Punta Herrero, in the *Sian Ka'an*, to *Xcalak*, near Belize."

"It's a natural paradise!"

"Two hours from the coast is the Chinchorro Bank, the largest coral atoll in America."

"Where does this beach road go?"

"First to El Uvero, a spot for fishing and diving. Then it goes to Río Indio, where we can camp and go kayaking or boating. There are still places like this on the Mayan Coast: rustic, without big hotels around."

"That's how I like it! Nature in its pure state."

"Wait 'til you see *Mahahual*, a paradise so little known that it only started to appear on maps 20 years ago. The beach, close to the coral reef, sparkles like emeralds."

"Let's go! Let's go!"

"Everyone wants to see Mahahual; its lighthouse guides the cruises that arrive each week to experience the primitive charm of the place."

"What's *Xcalak*?"

"A fishing village with beautiful beaches, a paradise for diving and sport fishing. It was born in 1900 as a military post during the Caste War. In 1955 Hurricane Janet almost wiped it off the map, but in the last few years it has made a strong comeback as a tourist destination."

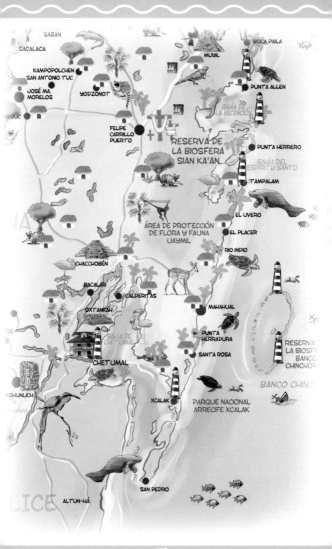

SABÁN
SACALACA
KAMPOLCHEN
SAN ANTONIO TUC
JOSÉ Ma.
MORELOS
YODZONOT
OYUC
FELIPE
CARRILLO
PUERTO

MUYIL
BOCA PAILA
PUNTA ALLEN
BAHÍA DE
LA ASCENSIÓN

RESERVA DE
LA BIOSFERA
SIAN KA'AN
PUNTA HERRERO
BAHÍA DEL
ESPÍRITU SANTO
TAMPALAM

ÁREA DE PROTECCIÓN
DE FLORA Y FAUNA
UAYMIL
EL UVERO
EL PLACER
RIO INDIO

CHACCHOBÉN
BACALAR
CALDERITAS
OXTANKAH
MAHAHUAL

BAHÍA DE
CHETUMAL
CHETUMAL
PUNTA
HERRADURA
SANTA ROSA
RESERVA
LA BIOSFE
BANCO
CHINCHOR

KOHUNLICH
BANCO CHINC

XCALAK
PARQUE NACIONAL
ARRECIFE XCALAK

ALTUN-HÁ
SAN PEDRO

LICE

Caribbean grand slam

"Why is there so much talk about sport fishing in Quintana Roo?"

"Because of its privileged geographical position. Did you know you don't have to travel miles and miles in order to fish here?"

"Really?"

"That's why this Association has been formed, uniting over 15 sport fishing committees throughout the State.

They all abide by a single set of regulations, for more responsible sport fishing, protecting the sailfish, and releasing blue marlin under the official size limit."

"That's good news."

"Better news is that they're encouraging "fishing tourism" in the State, promoting our tournaments at an international level."

"The folklore of Quintana Roo has influences from three regions, each with its own characteristics."

"Three regions?"

"In the north it shares history and traditions with the State of Yucatan, and you can see this in their dances, festivals and gastronomy."

"Do they eat panuchos and salbutes there too?"

"In the central region the Mayan community has preserved its traditions, and provides the purest example of the Mayan legacy, in music, like the *Maya pax*, their costumes, dances and the songs used in the religious celebrations with which their ancestors used to honor gods like *Chaac*, the god of rain, or the ceiba, the sacred tree."

"The center of Quintana Roo has a Mayan heart!"

"In the southern region, with a more recent

Culture and traditions

population, the principal music is *brukdown*, brought from Belize by the first inhabitants of Chetumal. It became the *Zambay* or zambo music festival, although today you can also hear *Reggae* and *Calypso*, the rhythms of the Caribbean."

"Are there carnivals?"

"Carnival is a legacy of colonial times. It's celebrated on major catholic religious dates. One traditional dance is that of the gum-tappers, peasants who went deep into the jungle in search of the sapodilla tree from which they obtained the gum."

"What about handcrafts?"

"On the coast they make them with shells. Elsewhere in the area they weave hammocks and make objects from wood and *guaco*."

Mayan Rituals

"Almost all of them have something to do with cultivating the land."

"And *Hanal Pixán*?"

"That's the exception. *Hanal Pixán* means "meal for the souls", and it's a Mayan tradition to honor our dead. It's celebrated each year at **Xcaret** Park. Setting up the altars, making the food, drink and sweets that our deceased liked, all brings us closer to them again."

"What other important rituals are there?"

"*Piibinal*, a ritual to prepare an offering to *Chaac*, god of rain."

"I know it: they choose corn cobs and bury them in a pit oven called a pib. They go dark, with a delicious smoked flavor."

"The ritual of praying for rain is called the *Ch'a Cháak*. There's another one called Janlikool, which is celebrated between January and March, and it's a meal for the gods who participated in the sowing of crops. The *Jo'osaj* is a religious ceremony to give thanks that the fields are on their way to a good harvest."

"How grateful the Mayan communities are!"

"They have so much religious fervor and respect for ancestral beliefs, that a bad harvest is attributed to lack of devotion and joy."

"I've heard of one very special one: the *Okol Bat'an*."

"It's a ceremony to bring the tithe to the church, so that God will provide the harvest. They offer food called *ts'an chakbi kaax* or chicken in broth."

"The Mayan world is alive in the 21st century!"

"The *Wajil kool* or "bread of the field" ritual is a ceremony praying for the owner of the field being worked, where you can see religious syncretism."

"In **Xel-Há** they perform the Honeybee or *Xunaan Cab* ceremony, in honor of the Mayan stingless bee."

"It's performed twice a year. A Mayan priest officiates, blessing and giving thanks for the production of honey."

"We have such a wealth of culture!"

Gastronomy

"So much traveling, admiring and learning has made me hungry."

"The gastronomy of Quintana Roo is that of the Peninsula, with dishes that reflect the mixture of ingredients and flavors from Spanish and Mayan cultures."

"My mouth's watering!"

"Mine too, just imagining the aroma of relleno negro, the taste of habanero chili, *x-catik* chili, ground pumpkin seed, annatto, *chaya* leaves, *x-pelón* beans. Mmm!"

"And what about cochinita *pibil*?"

"And relleno blanco, *papadzules*, *dzotobichay*, or *tikin-xic*, my goodness!"

"Let's go and try some of the delicacies of Quintana Roo!"

Handcrafts

"The artisans of Quintana Roo work wonders with local materials such as coconut, shells, wood, gourds and *cocoyol* seeds."

"What beautiful embroidery!"

"It's a tradition in Quintana Roo. For example, we have these beautiful *hipiles*. At **Xcaret** Park there are examples in the Museum of Popular Art at the Sisal Hacienda...There are some beautiful things!"

"What other handcrafts does the State have?

"On the coast they work with shells. Gum tapping and chewing gum manufacture is a traditional activity, which is still carried on in communities of Quintana Roo. The artisans of Felipe Carrillo make traditional musical instruments like *tunkules* that imitate the sounds of birds and monkeys."

"The hammocks they make in Santa Rosa, near Felipe Carrillo Puerto, are lovely."

Traditional Dances

"Are there a lot of dances in Quintana Roo?"
"Among traditional dances there are The Procession, a religious dance; the Pig's Head Dance, a pre-Hispanic dance which was offered to the gods. The pasacalle and the *calabaceado* are ballroom dances from the mid-20th century. The *fandango* from Spain is a happy dance that combines sones with jarana steps."
"The Quintana Roo jarana is a fusion of native, religious and secular; it has agile footwork and the waltz rhythm of the Aragonese jota."
"The *Sambay Macho* is a dance of resistance, and the Potpourri is a combination of regional dances."
"There is Mayan music and dance known as the festive or jarana Maya pax, which we can see in the **Xcaret** show, along with other traditional dances from our country."

Festivals

"Let's go to the festivals of Quintana Roo!"

"The best-known festival in the State is Carnival, which is celebrated before Lent, in February or March, in all the municipalities."

"So let's go to the carnival!"

"In several municipalities, especially in the Mayan region and Cozumel, they celebrate Holy Cross on the 3rd of May. They also observe religious festivals such as the Day of the Dead on the 31st of October and the 1st and 2nd of November. In **Xcaret** Park we can see the traditional Life and Death Festival. The Three Kings are remembered on the 6th of January, and several towns celebrate their patron saint."

"What about traditional festivals?"

"In the municipalities of the Mayan area they celebrate religious festivals with traditional roots, such as the *Lol Cah*, in which the village is blessed with Mayan prayers; the Sowing of the ceiba, the sacred tree; offerings to the god of rain, *Chaac*, to prevent droughts, and so on."

A serenade with flowers and song

"It's a festival for the Virgin of Guadalupe!"

"Every year **Xcaret** Park honors the Dark Virgin of Tepeyac with a lovely festival full of flowers and song. It starts after noon of the 11th of December and continues until dawn the next day."

"The Chapel of Guadalupe in **Xcaret** is decorated with flowers, and outside there are beautiful altars with chrysanthemums, Easter lilies and sprays of gypsophila."

"The arrival of the torch-bearers cues the first liturgies and praying the rosary."

"It's a religious festival beyond description. The people of the community sing a serenade and remember the apparitions of the Dark Virgin on Tepeyac Hill."

Mayan Crossing

"And all these rowers?"

"They are getting ready for the crossing to Cozumel on Thursday, Friday and Saturday in the second half of May. It's a re-enactment of the ancient ritual pilgrimage which the peoples of the Yucatan Peninsula made to the port of *Polé,* now **Xcaret**, in order to take a boat for *Cuzamil,* now Cozumel, to worship the goddess *Ix Chel* and to consult her oracle, which was the only one in the region."

"How many canoes are there?"

"There are 30 canoes 26 feet long, crewed by ten rowers, who cross the Cozumel Channel both 11 miles each way."

"A real spectacle!"

"The re-enactment of the Sacred Mayan Crossing was an initiative of **Xcaret** Park, in coordination with the municipalities of Cozumel and Solidaridad. It recaptures the memory carved in glyphs and recorded by chroniclers of the Indies."

"Where are all these people going?"

"You mean, where are we going? We're going to the **Xel-Há** Sprint and Olympic Triathlon. It's a great project that links a Natural Marvel like **Xel-Há** with sport and physical activity."

"What have you got me into this time?"

"The natural park at **Xel-Há** organizes an international-level sports meet, backed by the Mexican Triathlon Federation."

"Are you sure we can participate?"

"Of course! It's also backed by private enterprise to foster sport in our region."

"In what sport or category are we going to participate?"

"The trial is open to specialist triathletes and cyclists, swimmers and sportspeople in general, from nine years old to over 60."

"Fine, I'll be OK with the fifteen-year-olds."

"Don't flatter yourself! Better come and see the starting line."

"The floating bridge! Just at the estuary where the main inlet of the natural park joins the waters of the Caribbean. This is going to be good!"

"This is just the beginning. Hurry up, who knows, we might even win."

X Trips to see unforgettable places in the Southeast of Mexico

"*Xcaret Xperiences*? What's that?"

"That's the name of the luxury tours to some incredible places in the Yucatan peninsula."

"Luxury?"

"Yes. To *Chichén Itzá*, Wonder of the World; to Valladolid, colonial jewel; to Izamal, one of Mexico's magical places; to *Tulum, Cobá* and *Ek' Balam*, mysterious Mayan cities."

"You can't know the southeast of Mexico without visiting these historic places!"

Tours

"And other beautiful ecological sites, like Ría Lagartos, where flamingoes live in their natural habitat."
"How are we going to see so much on one tour?"
"There are guides at all the sites, and time to enjoy the gastronomic specialties of each place."
"Mmm! Delicious Valladolid pork in tomato sauce!"
"It's a new concept in tours, to get to know unforgettable places in the Southeast of Mexico."

Valladolid

"Valladolid was founded on the 28th of May 1543, by Francisco de Montejo, the Nephew, on a site known as *Chouac-há*. Later it was moved to the town of *Zací*, a Mayan word that means "white sparrow hawk". But the conquistadores did not have it easy: Cupules and *Choues*, the Mayan groups that inhabited the area, fought them fiercely."

"You can see it was an important city."

"So important that it was the epicenter of the

conquest of the eastern Peninsula."

"And once the region was conquered, what happened?"

"Lands were handed out to the encomenderos, the Church began to build churches and monasteries, and civil and administrative buildings were erected."

"Did the Caste War come this way?"

"In 1848, Valladolid was taken by the Maya under Cecilio *Chí*."

"And the white and mestizo population?"

"They were evicted, but many died in the conflict. The devastated city was in the hands of the rebels for several months until the army of the governor Miguel Barbachano retook it."

"What happened after the Caste War?"

"Listen to this: the first revolutionary movement in Mexico sprang up in Valladolid. It was in June 1910, and in Yucatan it's known as "the first spark of the Revolution"."

"What can you tell me about the architecture?"

"There's plenty to say about that: to start with, there's the famous Cathedral of St. Gervase."

"Very impressive, and on the Main Square!"

"Construction began in 1543. In the 18th

century it was the scene of a bloody crime, and as a way to make amends, the facade was reoriented towards the north, whereas the custom was for it to face east."

"You mean the entrance wasn't the one we see now?"

"The portico was conserved as you see it, with the sculptures of St. Peter and St. Paul."

"Such beautiful colonial streets. And this monastery?"

"It's the ex-monastery of St. Bernardino of Siena, the first seat of the Franciscan Order in Valladolid."

"It looks like a medieval fortress."

"It was built in 1552, in the heart of the old Sisal quarter. Inside there is a beautiful wooden altarpiece with gold chasing, and in the ground floor passageway, going out towards the monastery orchard, there is an old noria over a cenote."

"The Friars' Walkway is spectacular!"

"And what about "**La Casona**"? You can enjoy the architecture and the wide range of Yucatecan dishes."

"Let's walk. The colonial streets, houses and plazas of Valladolid are beautiful, although when it comes to a stroll, there's nothing like the Candelaria quarter."

"Where's the church?"

"The Candelaria Church and the old Candelaria prison are now the Pedro Saínz de Baranda Public Library. Here's an interesting piece of trivia: the first loom in Mexico was installed right here, in 1835. What do you reckon?"

"Marvelous!"

"Well there are more marvels waiting for you in Valladolid now we wander through the traditional quarters of Santa Ana, San Juan and Santa Lucía with their churches and plazas, where the locals still get together."

"And the cenotes? They tell me there are a lot."

"You mustn't miss them. The best-known are Zací, a really impressive cenote, and Dzitnup, with its color and beauty beyond words."

"We've walked a long way!"

"And we still haven't seen City Hall, the handcrafts market and the San Roque Museum, which houses important documents from our history."

Izamal
Magical Town

"I've always wanted to see Izamal with you!"
"Izamal comes from the Maya *Itzmal*, which means "dew from heaven". It's also known as the "city of the three cultures", because of its pre-Hispanic, colonial and contemporary Mexican heritage; and as the "city of the hills" because of its monumental pyramids."
"It was one of the great sites of Mayan culture!"
"Today you can still see the remains of the

great pyramids, and the network of roads or sacbés, that gives you an idea of the political and religious power of the city."

"Who founded Izamal?"

"Izamal was founded by the Itzaes around the year 550 AD. Their high priest, *Zamná*, adopted the name of the Mayan sun god, *Itzamná*."

"That's why their city was called Izamal!"

"It was abandoned during the Postclassical, before the arrival of the Spanish, but it remained a center of pilgrimage to venerate *Itzamná*."

"And did the Spanish like it like that, deserted?"

"So much so that the Franciscans decided to build the great Monastery of St. Anthony of Padua on top of one of the five pyramids."

"Five pyramids?"

"They're very large pyramids, but the outstanding one is *Kinich Kak Moo*."

"It's enormous!"

"It's a huge pyramid with ten levels, dedicated to a solar deity. It's visible from many parts of the city. It's 656 feet along each side, and 112 feet high!"

"It must have been an imposing city!"

"No doubt about it! Many of these monuments, and others in the area around Izamal, formed part of the lordship of *Ah Kin Chel*."

"And how were things here in the Colonial period?"

"How do you think? Everything was organized under the encomienda system, which lasted through the whole colonial period."

"And the famous monastery?"

"The Franciscan monastery of St Anthony of Padua is one of the most impressive 16th century religious complexes in all Mexico."

"It's different from a lot of monasteries I know."

"It's a living example of how the Maya were evangelized."

"Why?"

"The Maya performed their rituals in the open air; to introduce them to the Church it was necessary to have transitional open spaces."

"That's why this atrium is so big?"

"It's the largest closed atrium in Mexico, almost as big as that of St. Peter's in Rome. Evangelization was also served by the open chapel on the facade and the processional corridor with its 75 arches through which the natives could reach the posa (processional) chapels, where they were taught the sacraments."

"Who is this statue of?"

"Fray Diego de Landa, bishop of Yucatan, a Franciscan friar who lived here. He directed construction of the monastery, which began in 1553 and terminated, together with the church, in 1561. This friar brought from Guatemala the image of the Virgin of the Immaculate Conception, queen and patroness of Yucatan."

"Fray Diego de Landa? That name rings a bell..."

"Of course it does! He was the one who burnt the sacred books of the Maya in the famous "auto da fé" at Maní."

"Of course! They prosecuted him, and in his defense he wrote the "Account of Things of Yucatan"."

"What a paradox! He's the only direct source for the study of the ancient Maya."

"Izamal still has its colonial downtown."

"Come on, let's have a ride in that horse-buggy."

"What a lovely ride!"

"Did you know that there's a light and sound show in the evenings, in the atrium of the monastery?"

"Of course, and we mustn't miss it! Even Pope John Paul II went to see it."

Chichén Itzá
Wonder of the World

"What an amazing site"

"*Chichén Itzá* means "at the mouth of the well of the *Itzaes*", and refers to the Sacred Cenote at the city, which was a Mayan capital between 900 and 1400 AD."

"Is the city old?"

"It was built between 435 and 455 AD, in the *Puuc* and *Chenes* architectural styles. The first Itzaes arrived around 968 to 987 AD. They came from the lowlands of Tabasco, and brought with them Toltec cultural influences from central Veracruz, Tabasco and Xochicalco."

"Where can you see it?"

"In the Yucatecan Maya style of buildings like the Pyramid of *Kukulkán*."

"When did the city decline?"

"In the early 15th century, with the fall of Mayapan as a political center, *Chichén Itzá* was depopulated, and remained forgotten in the jungle for centuries."

"Is that how the Spanish found it?"

1 Sacred Cenote
2 Ball Court
3 *Tzompantli*
4 Platform of Eagles and Jaguars
5 Platform of Venus
6 Castle
7 Temple of the Warriors
8 Market
9 Steam Bath
10 Plaza of the Thousand Columns
11 Temple of the Large Tables
12 *Xtoloc* Cenote
13 Ossuary
14 *Chichanchob* or Red House
15 Hause of the Deer
16 Caracol or Observatory
17 Temple of the Panels
18 House of the Nuns
19 Church
20 *Akab Dzib*

"Yes. By the time they arrived, the glory days of great *Chichén Itzá* had passed."

The Castle
or Pyramid of Kukulcán

"I've seen a thousand photos of it: it's impressive."

"It's a masterpiece of Mayan architecture. It measures 182 feet along each side and is 79 feet high, including the last of its nine stepped sections, the staircases on each side and a temple at the summit."

"When did they build it?"

"In *Chichén Itzá*'s glory days, when Mayapán dominated the region."

"Look at the size of those staircases!"

"The balustrades end in two colossal heads of plumed serpents, effigies of the god Kukulcán."

"And the temple has columns in the form of snakes."

"Did you know that this pyramid is built on top of another smaller one?"

"Really?"

"Inside they found a red jaguar with jade inlays, which was used as a throne by the *Halach Uinic*."

"Is it true that the design encapsulates much of the Maya's knowledge of the calendar?"

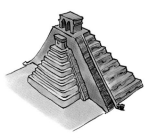

"Each step on the staircases is a day of the year. There are four sides and as each side has 91 steps, that gives a total of 364. If you add the platform at the top, you get the 365 days of the solar year."

"And also it's dedicated to *Kukulkán*."

"If you look at just one side, the corners of the nine sections total 18, which are the 20-day months of the solar of *Haab* calendar."

"Gulp!"

"The 260 quadrangles on the platforms are the number of days in the *Tzolkín*, which was the lunar calendar."

"It also indicates the movement of the rotation of the earth and the heavenly bodies."

"The Mayan astronomers built this

pyramid in such a way
that during the equinoxes it
coincides with the elliptic."
"The elliptiwhat?"
"During the equinoxes, when their
orientation produces the descent of *Kukulcán*."
"What's this Descent of *Kulkulcán*?"
"The plumed serpent that comes down from the
summit."
"You're kidding me!"
"In March and September, on the spring and
autumn equinoxes, the corners of the platforms
of the pyramid project a shadow which forms
isosceles triangles of light on the balustrade on
the north side of the pyramid. This creates the
illusion of the body of a snake descending from
the top, and appearing to move downwards,
ending in the serpent's head at the bottom of the
balustrade."

The Ball Court

"The Ball Game, known as pok ta pok in the Mayan region, was played all over Mesoamerica."

"Were there a lot of ball courts?"

"Very many. Over 2000. At *Chichén Itzá* alone there were about ten, but none as monumental as this one. It's 551 feet long and 230 feet wide, shaped like a capital I. You can see the game being played every day at **Xcaret** Park."

"What are those things embedded in the walls?"

"They're decorated stone rings. Apparently you had to make the ball go through them."

"And those temples?"

"They're religious temples for the dignitaries. The game was a big ritual event."

... HE'S AN OVERSEAS PLAYER, SIR...

"This temple looks like a copy of one I saw at Tula: the Temple of *Tlahuizcalpantecuhtli*."

"Well this may come as a surprise, but it's the other way round. The Tula one is almost identical to the Temple of Warriors here, because it was the Maya who influenced the inhabitants of Tula."

"Did you see the staircase?"

"It leads to the upper temple, with an entrance formed by two rattlesnake columns."

"They say there was an earlier temple underneath."

"It's known as the Temple of the *Chac Mool*, because of the *Chac Mool* which they found there."

"And these huge columns at the base of the temple?"

"They're pilasters that used to hold up a great hall. They have carved figures that recreate a procession of dignitaries."

"I loved the *Chac mool*!"

"Stand there and I'll take a photo."

The Observatory or Caracol

"What's this? It looks like an observatory."

"It's the Observatory or Caracol ("Snail"), one of the most original buildings in the Mayan world."

"They're almost never round."

"This building was constructed during the first Military City period. It's a broad circular tower standing on a platform."

"Yes, I see."

"The tower has three superimposed structures: the first level is a circular base; the second is a frieze decorated with a mask of *Chaac* and a seated figure; and the third, which is much deteriorated, still has the openings for making astronomical observations."

"Did the Maya know about astronomy?"

"Did they what? They calculated the length of the solar year and predicted eclipses with an exactness that still astounds scientists today."

Ek´ Balam

"We're in the Mayan city of *Ek´Balam*, which means "Star Jaguar" or "Black Jaguar". This white road, or sacbé, will take us into this beautiful city, once surrounded by walls."

"Wow! Everything's so big! It must have been an important city."

"Ek´ Balam is to the north of the colonial city of Valladolid. It was inhabited in the early 300s AD, but its period of greatest growth was in the Late Classical and Terminal Classical periods (500 - 1000 AD)."

"It's very large, and the buildings are monumental."

"The plaza of the city is flanked by mounds and large platforms that are still being excavated."

"But I can see some big, beautifully decorated buildings."

"Yes. There are temples and vaulted palaces with well-preserved facades and murals that tell us how important this city was, especially in the Classical period, for example the main temple known as the Acropolis or Structure 1."

"Murals? What's in the murals?"

"In the murals there are inscriptions painted or carved on the stone, which tell us the history of the first recorded king, *Ukit Kan Le´k Tok´* or "father of the four faces of flint" by name."

"Ahhh, now I remember... the founder of an apparently very powerful dynasty."

"Yes. Their base was the city of *Ek´ Balam*. That

big building you see there, the Acropolis, is
thought to be their tomb."

"Look at the huge entrance to it. It looks like
the mouth of a monster. It's called *Sak Xok Naah*
which means "The white house of reading"."

"Yes, and it represents the entrance to the
underworld. But there is also the Oval Building,
the Ball Court, the sculptures and stelae that
have managed to survive the ravages of time.
Little by little we are learning more details of the
history of this monumental Mayan city."

Ría Lagartos

"It's called a "ría" or estuary, because it looks like a river, although because of its depth it's also considered a marsh."

"How long has it been known?"

"In their 16th century chronicles, the Spanish conquistadores mentioned this inlet from the sea on the north coast of the Yucatan Peninsula."

"I see it's an environmental reserve."

"This area, which was declared a "biosphere reserve" in 1979, is bigger than the inlet itself, and covers 233 square miles, where over 250 species of water birds reproduce."

"Is the inlet enclosed on all sides?"

"This body of water is partially enclosed. It connects with the Gulf of Mexico, and receives

fresh water from springs and outflows on dry land."

"There's life everywhere!"

"It's called biodiversity, and it's created by the abundance of mangroves and the fauna they protect, with so many birds, reptiles and fish that I can't find the words to explain its extraordinary wealth."

"Look! Those beautiful pink birds are...er..."

"They're Mexican flamingoes!"

"I'd only ever heard about them. I never thought I'd see them up close."

"Ría Lagartos is their natural habitat, that's why you can see them everywhere. I'd like to tie one by the feet and bring it to you."

"Don't even think about it! I don't want to see you carried off in the attempt."

You must'nt miss...

"We've seen the best of Quintana Roo, but our journey would be incomplete if we didn't make these visits to **Xcaret, Xplor** and **Xel-Há,** ecological parks that safeguard the natural wonders of the region."

"Is there anything else to amaze us?"

"You're going to experience the beauty of the Caribbean Sea, the exuberance of nature, the most beautiful natural aquarium and the unforgettable experience of entering the heart of the Earth."

"What are you talking about?"

"About **Xcaret**, a natural area with endless activities, places immersed in Mayan culture and

contact with the flora and fauna of the region."

"And **Xel-Há**?"

"It's a sacred paradise and the most beautiful natural aquarium in the world."

"What are we waiting for?"

"Let's go! On the way I'll tell you about **Xplor,** a place for adventures in caves and excitement for all the family. And we can't miss *Tulum*, the Mayan world on a single site."

"Can we go to several places on the same day?"

"Of course! There are combined trips: **Xel-Há** - *Tulum*, *Tulum* - **Xel-Há** - **Xcaret** (The Night-time Spectacle)."

"This is Xcaret, Mexico's great ecological park."
"And one of the best in the world. **Xcaret** is a world of nature and culture. It's a reencounter with our vital essence."
"In the past it was the Mayan port of *Polé*."
"Look! We can swim with dolphins!"
"And with sharks and rays. We can even take an underwater trip."
"Really?"
"And that's not to mention all the natural marvels we can find at **Xcaret.**"
"Tell me! Tell me about them!"
"We can see jaguars in their natural habitat, and all kinds of animals, some

of them endangered, like the tapir and the manatee."

"Look at the macaws overhead."

"There are more than 40 species of bird in their natural habitat. There's a beautiful butterfly house and a coral reef aquarium you'll never forget."

"Turtles!"

"Marine turtles, endangered today, have a special place at **Xcaret**."

"This place is like a dream."

"There are caves, underground rivers, turquoise beaches and trails full of natural beauty."

"And are those real Mayan temples?"

"They're archaeological remains of the ancient port of *Polé*. At **Xcaret,** history comes to life: the Mayan people sink their roots into the pre-Hispanic world, the beautiful Chapel of St. Francis takes us back to the colonial past, and the Sisal Hacienda transports us to the golden age of sisal cultivation in the Peninsula."

"Mexico can be seen everywhere here!"

"In the Mexican cemetery you can experience the very essence of popular culture in this country, in the ingenious epitaphs engraved on the colorful tombs."

"Where are all these people going?"
"To "**Xcaret** Mexico Spectacular." It's an event where the protagonist is Mexico, a country that overflows with cultural identity, with over 300 performers on stage."
"It's a park like few others in the world."
"It's unique, and now you know it, let's experience it!"
"Let's live the **Xcaret** experience!"

"**Xplor** is an underground park that is unique in the Caribbean!"

"Are they caves? It all looks so exciting: cables going up and down."

"It's an extraordinary sample of Quintana Roo's geography. The formation of huge caves through the erosion of limestone has left an underground landscape of great beauty."

"I feel as if I'm in a movie about cavemen. Just so long as no dinosaurs show up!"

"According to geological studies, the formation of caves and cenotes in the Yucatan Peninsula is connected to the porosity of the rock, which allows water to filter through. Over millions of years this erodes the rock and creates caverns, caves and cenotes."

"That explains why it's so fascinating!"

"At **Xplor** we are privileged to descend into the bowels of the Earth."

"Not a very dignified descent with all this stuff they've put on me. I don't want to imagine what a caveman would think if he saw me."
"This safety equipment is state-of-the-art, the best and safest in the world."

"Where do we start?"

"The Xplor experience is unique: from diving into a sea of stalactites and stalagmites, to driving an amphibious vehicle underground, through water and jungle, then sailing a raft along underground rivers, and a splashdown after a fantastic flight above the jungle on an zip line."

"All that?"

"I told you: Xplor is unique. There are four different activities: a zip line with a splashdown in a cenote; rafting; swimming in an underground river and the tour in an amphibious vehicle. What's the matter?"

"We haven't started and I'm tired already, and hungry and thirsty… Let me sit here for a moment."

"Hungry and thirsty isn't a problem! We can spend an amazing day here and enjoy the finest healthy food and drink, designed by specialized

nutritionists."

"Everything I see looks incredible! How do these amazing structures happen underground?"

"These caves experience a very special phenomenon. The upper layer is fresh water, rainwater that because of its density floats on top of the seawater that filters through the porous rock."

"And the stalactites and stalagmites?"

"They're natural formations made of calcium carbonate and other minerals, produced by water filtration over hundreds of thousands of years."

"I feel as if I'm on another planet, and that's without everything we can do in this wonderful park."

"It's fun and adventure in a natural setting, to feel the intensity of living."

"Are you talking about the zip line?"

"I'm talking about everything! Get in. Although the zip line experience is unique and safe, nothing compares to these amphibious vehicles."

"It's like in the movies! We can go over bridges, into caves and underground rivers in this vehicle. It's so much fun!"

"And what about the zip line? Off you go!"

"D…do I h…have to?"

"And miss out on the adrenalin of flying 3,600 yards above the jungle?"

"3,600 yards?"

"You can jump off on any of the lines, pass through the different towers and finally

splashdown in a beautiful cenote."
"I only understood half of what you said. But it sounds so wonderful and exciting, that I want to jump off any tower you want and splashdown on any suspension bridge you tell me."
"You're still confused!"
"The important thing is that we're well protected by our equipment. What's important is that no cavemen appear, they'd be so scared to see me that they'd never evolve."
"And if you want to relax, there's nothing better than a trip on one of these rafts that take us through a world of caverns."
"I'm never going to forget this experience, I can promise you that."

"**Xel-Há**, a paradise on the Mayan Riviera."
"It's…it's beautiful!"
"It's the loveliest natural aquarium in the World,
a Mexican natural marvel and an experience
of beauty and harmony. It's the mouth of the
longest underground river in the world: the *Sac
Actun* system."

"Look at the color of the water!"

"The main feature of **Xel-Há** is this inlet where the water from a river joins the Caribbean Sea, creating the perfect habitat for 90 marine and freshwater species to live together."

"Is it true that **Xel-Há** is protected by the gods?"

"The legend relates that the gods created **Xel-Há** when they wanted to see the best of themselves in one place. To protect it they created three guardians: *Huh*, the iguana, guardian of earth; *Chuc Kay*, the pelican, guardian of the sky; and *Kay-Op*, the parrot fish, of the waters."

"What can you do at **Xel-Há**?"

"What do you want to do? This place has everything!"

THE DOLPHINS AT XEL-HÁ

"Let's go into the inlet."

"It's an open-air aquarium where you can see over 70 maritime species. Sometimes you can even see the pink conch, a protected species at **Xel-Há**."

"Look! Dolphins!"

"Do you want to swim with them? You can swim with the manatee too."

"I want to do everything. Let's go down that path."

"All the paths at **Xel-Há** take you to landscapes, mammals, reptiles and birds of every color."

"And plants!"

"Of **Xel-Há**'s 207 acres, 158 are tropical jungle. There are more than 220 species of plants!"

"Here's to adventure!"

"Travel through the **Xel-Há** river, cross the Floating Bridge, cross the Rope Bridge, try the zip line, try the aerial bike and jump from the Rock

THE INLET

SEA TREK

ROPE BRIDGE

of Courage!"
"I'm flabbergasted!"
"You haven't seen anything.
You have to discover the
mystery of the cenotes, the
El Dorado Cave with its
marine fossils, the Maya
Cave, the *Ix Chel* Cave and
the Mayan Wall."
"Hammocks!"
"This is Hammock Island."
"Wonderful!"
"They've been used by
the Maya for centuries.
Swinging in a hammock is
like floating on air."
"Let's see everything the
park has to offer, then come
and float on Hammock
Island."
"That way we'll be sure
that **Xel-Há** isn't just a
dream, but a living reality
in the Mexican Caribbean
Passport."

ROCK OF COURAGE

BICYCLE ROUTE

SWIM WITH DOLPHINS

FLOATING BRIDGE

About the author

Covo

JAVIER COVO TORRES
(www.javiercovo.com)
Born Cartagena, Colombia, 1958

Architectural restorer and artist specializing in the history of art, the author admits to being a cartoonist, in which guise he has written – and illustrated – dozens of humorous books, following the old adage of "make learning fun."

Mayan World Series

The Maya on the Rocks
Maya Sutra
Mayamerón
Calendario maya (sin estrés)
El libro maya de los porqués
El libro maya de los acertijos
Las profecías mayas
Los dioses mayas (para idólatras)
Popol Vuh (para principiantes)
Leyendas mayas

Yucatan Series

Bombas Yucatecas
Pasaporte Yucateco

Biographies Series

Einstein (relativamente fácil)
Freud (para inconscientes)
Mozart (ma non troppo)
Beethoven (para sordos)
Van Gogh (para esquizoides)
Picasso (en cubitos)
Leonardo da Vinci (al fresco)
Gandhi (en ayunas)
Napoleón (a la mignón)
Julio César (a lo bruto)

Other titles

El arte de la guerra
El viaje de Colón
Ajedrez (juego demente)
Pasaporte Xcaret

An indispensable identity document in the Mexican Caribbean

A unique experience!

MEXICAN CARIBBEAN PASSPORT
1st Edition, 2012, Quintana Roo.
ISBN: 978-607-00-5046-6
Printed in Singapore

TEXT, DESIGN AND ILLUSTRATIONS:
Javier Covo Torres

LAYOUT:
Cobá Divulgaciones S.A. de C.V.

TECHNICAL REVISION:
Ileana Reyes Campos

LOGISTICAL SUPPORT:
Libia Franco González

TRANSLATION:
David Phillips/ Kathy Loretta

Xcaret Experiences Collection